T0149409

FINDING JOY

ELLEN PAYNE

BALBOA.
PRESS

A DIVISION OF HAY HOUSE

Balboa Press books may be ordered through booksellers or by contacting:

Balboa Press
A Division of Hay House
1663 Liberty Drive
Bloomington, IN 47403
www.balboapress.com.au
1 (877) 407-4847

Print information available on the last page.

ISBN: 978-1-5043-0760-4 (sc)
ISBN: 978-1-5043-0768-0 (e)

Balboa Press rev. date: 04/12/2017

Dedicated to survivors of abuse.

INTRODUCTION

"I cannot teach anyone anything. I can only make them think"
Socrates

"Who, what and why am I?" are things that Joy has been wondering, off and on, for most of her life. She has been on a quest to find herself for many years; wanting to know this person, to whom she is so intimately connected. She has felt that she doesn't fit easily into whom or what others expect her to be. She certainly hasn't found it easy to behave as others seem to have expected her to behave. What value did she have when she apparently caused her parents so much heartache, disappointed her teachers, was a mediocre wife and mother, received less pay than her male colleagues, had to resign from paid employment when she married and needed her husband's permission to open a bank account?

Those days have passed but still there have been lingering doubts about her value. Does one have to justify one's existence? Is it enough when you come to the end of life, to be able to say that your achievements outweigh your regrets?

Some comments people made have stuck in her mind. "She should have been a boy." "She isn't like the others." "There's not much of her father's family in her." Names that she was called like, "Number Two", "Fat", "Bath Tub" and "Wife" have impacted on her psyche and helped to define her. Into this mix have been added things that have happened to her giving her more labels like "victim", "survivor", "striver" and "thriver". Joy is a woman, daughter, sister, mum, auntie, grandma and friend. Things that she has achieved were also added. She was a Queen's Guide, Occupational Therapist and eventually a Minister of religion. Now she is 'elderly' and retired with beginning signs of dementia. But do any or even all of these things really say who she is? Isn't a person more than the sum of such tags?

Joy feels that each label is attached to a box into which she is expected to neatly fit but she knows that boxes are constricting by nature. They are constructed by cultural and community ideas, teaching and expectations. Adding more boxes may seem like a good thing; giving more labels - but many things that define also confine.

Any definition is, by its nature, limiting. It can only say in part who someone is; something that Joy tries to remember when she is tempted to label others. But Joy has found that the more she has been able to answer the question, "Who do *I* say that I am?" the more complete her life has become. Coming to recognise what she has learned, to know her strengths when all she had seen in herself were weaknesses, her achievements as well as her failures, has freed her of a huge burden and allowed her to live her life more fully. Accepting herself has helped her to accept others for who they are and to be less judgemental in her attitudes. She is much more at peace with the answers that she so far has than she was previously.

Joy recognises that her understandings are still evolving. She may be well past "middle age" but still has a way to go on what has been an incredible journey with its many highs and lows.

It is her hope that her story will encourage others who may be undertaking such a journey to self- discovery and those who are wary of risking the first step. If you are already on such an adventure, be encouraged to keep going and don't give up when the inevitable hard, painful times occur because it will be worthwhile in the end.

Joy has chosen for her story to be written under a pseudonym at the request of her sisters who are concerned by the probable repercussions of their partners and families learn their secrets.

QUESTIONS, QUESTIONS

"We can easily forgive a child who is afraid of the dark; the real tragedy of life is when [people] are afraid of the light." Socrates

As was her habit, Joy had the television on to catch up with the news while she ate breakfast. She had just about finished eating when they began to interview a priest who had given evidence to the Royal Commission on Child Sexual Abuse in Institutions that was currently in progress. Joy watched him for a couple of minutes then she jumped to her feet, switching off the television as she did so. She flung the remote on to the chair on which she had been sitting.

"I can't bear to watch him a moment longer," she cried to the empty room. "He is so unmoved. Why doesn't he get how much it has hurt the children? Why can't he show a little humility? Then we could see that he *means* that he is sorry for the pain that people have suffered. Even if he wasn't actually responsible for the abuse, the institution he represents was and that should have some influence on his feelings. It isn't that this particular priest has turned a blind eye to the abuse. He seemed to have known that it was happening. It is just irrelevant to him. He can't see anything wrong with it or how it can have hurt anyone. He has no compassion for the victims."

In Joy's mind, those who knew the abuse was happening and did nothing, and those who denied there was any abuse, are as guilty, if not more so, as the actual perpetrators. What was that old saying? "The only thing it takes for evil to flourish is for good people to do nothing." Where it came from she didn't know but it did seem relevant to this situation. Many people have apparently known that abuse was happening and done nothing. "Can people be called 'good' when they turn a blind eye to the abuse of others?" she wondered.

"Can't this man see that he is adding to the agony of the victims? Why doesn't he get it? Why don't all of them get it? Could it possibly be that people who have not experienced abuse simply cannot understand, or is it that they dare not - that it is just too confronting for them? Maybe they have been abused and have buried the memories so that it is too painful to acknowledge that these things happen." The questions were going round and round in her head like clothes in a tumble drier the way they had done every time she heard or saw something in the media about the Royal Commission into Child Sexual Abuse in Institutions.

Joy remembered how her youngest sister, Lyn, had broken her leg playing "chasey" when she was four. "It was only a greenstick fracture," they said. Nevertheless the leg was in plaster for several weeks before it was healed. Later in anatomy lessons Joy had learnt that when a bone heals, it has a remarkable way of laying down new cells around the damage so that where it joins becomes stronger than the original bone. Lyn knew this too. She had needed an X-ray for a knee injury and had seen, on the edge of the film, the bulge in the bone in the area of original damage. If she lives to a hundred as her mother has, and has her leg X-rayed again, the scar of the wound would still be visible.

Mostly Lyn forgets that it had ever happened, but every now and then, even now in her sixties, something occurs to remind her of that wintry day all those years ago when the break had occurred. It might be that she had become very cold, or that she had bumped her leg, or that she had done some more strenuous exercise than usual. Then it would ache and the memory flooded back.

It was like that for Joy with some of the injuries she had sustained. Like Lyn's, hers had not been outwardly visible on her body, and she knows that she is stronger in some ways because of them, but unlike Lyn's, hers are not visible on any X-ray film. Her wounds have been mainly psychological. At the time they occurred, she didn't realise the lasting effects these wounds would have on her life. Nobody realised, or if they did, they did not acknowledged that she had been injured and so no remedial action had been taken for many years.

As the dull ache in her heart prompted memories to the surface, Joy's thoughts continued. "Perhaps some evils were too difficult or painful for some people to even begin to acknowledge so they are denied for self-preservation. I know that denial is a strong protective force when people feel helpless or unable to face reality. I have used it myself."

Sexual Abuse had been in the news daily but it still surprised Joy that agonising thoughts kept coming back to her. She thought she had dealt with all this years ago. With a heavy sigh, she sank back into the chair. She would be glad when the Royal Commission was over and the whole affair would be seen to have been dealt with by well-meaning folk. Any guilt Child Protection Authorities or the Church and other institutions had felt would be relieved [though one of the problems was that they didn't seem to feel any guilt]. The Commissioners and representatives of Institutions had done their duty and now they could get on with their lives without having to face this piece of the reality of some other people's existence.

Then Joy wouldn't hurt so much, when she wasn't constantly reminded that people like her mattered even less than those who had been sexually abused in institutions. Like many thousand others, Joy had suffered multiple abuses in her own home at the hands of her parents. None of them had been severe enough to come to the attention of authorities when she was growing up in the forties and fifties but they had marred her life and that of others she came in contact with, including her husband and children.

Joy knows from stories she has been told that there are many others who lived with the anger, shame, frustration, disappointment and even despair from their memories of abuse. Most live in silence with their secret, terrified of anyone ever finding out about them. Some have tried to talk about what happened only to find few people care. The response from others can be sceptical as Joy found to her cost. "I knew your family. I never saw your parents behaving like that. "You always were a problem child," one said, placing the blame on her.

When the abuse is no longer talked about daily on the media, Joy's emotions will subside and she will be able to push the memories back down into the cellars of her mind so that what she presents to the world is a relatively normal façade of decency and care. For now she must get on with what is needed to be done today and she turned her thoughts to that.

But it isn't only in the media that issues around abuse come up. Since the government has made laws requiring people in organisations and Churches who work with children to have *Working with Children* checks, ordinary people have been faced with thinking more about this issue. Some have refused to get their checks and others have seen themselves as being persecuted by the requirement. Those who have not experienced abuse speak out loudly, blaming victims, calling allegations malicious and refuse to believe anything against those accused.

Recently Joy had been talking to some people in such a position. A man who was unable to get a Working with Children Certificate because of convictions, had been working in their community with children for many years. Joy feared that during this time there may well have been more offences committed and she tried to persuade the people that there could be some other victims in their community who need their support and care. But they said that the claims made were false even though the person had pleaded guilty and received a sentence. They said that he had told them that he had done this to spare the embarrassment for the accuser of going through a trial and they admired him for this.

When Joy saw how fiercely they defended him, she was reminded of when someone had told her that you can't argue a person into changing their mind. No amount of arguing on her part would get these people to change theirs and so she just had to retreat, hoping that none of their children had been among his victims.

Joy went on with her breakfast, ashamed that yet again she had let her compassion for unrecognised victims overwhelm her. You might think that now she was in her seventies, it would be less of a bother. All the same, the response of the priest who was on the television, had hit a nerve. She tried to block the thoughts but found herself again smouldering with indignation. It wasn't only her, if the stories that she had heard first hand and the figures she had read were anything like accurate! There have to be hundreds of thousands of victims of sexual abuse whose dilemma has not been addressed by the Royal Commission. Its brief is too limited. People could not face the implications of widening the scope of the Commission. It would be humiliating for a nation that has prided itself on everyone getting "a fair go," to know more truths about abuse.

Statistics Joy had heard said that as many as one in two women and one in five men in Australia experience some form of sexual abuse at some stage in their lives.

The Royal Commission has only been looking into the *sexual abuse* of *children* in *institutions*. Sexual abuse rarely occurs in isolation. There are several other forms of abuse such as physical, verbal and emotional. Most people who have been abused may not have been children when it occurred. Many are vulnerable adults such as women with abusive partners and people with disabilities and have not suffered the abuse in institutions.

Joy had heard that sometimes now the term "Abuse" is replaced with the term "Violence" because the behaviour of one person has violated the other. The use of this other word is also an attempt to get the general public to take what is happening in our communities more seriously. This is now also the practice of some professional when talking about suicide. They say, "He killed himself" so that the starkness of this form of violence is better confronted.

Early on in the process of the Royal Commission, Joy had seen an article in a newspaper that she wishes now she had cut out and kept. It suggested that the parameters for the Commission were too narrow and that they should be broadened to include all people who had been sexually abused whatever the circumstances. The writer said that although this would be ideal, it was likely to take too many years for the Government to provide the funding.

That was the only time she has heard anyone suggest this. There seemed not to have been another trace of recognition anywhere she has seen or heard; that there might be many who did not fall in the guidelines of survivors given to the Royal Commission by the Government. Surely she is not the only one who thinks about these victims. There have to be others like her, not necessarily wanting the world to know their story but longing for some recognition that they have had their innocence taken from them, and their self-esteem and faith in humans shattered when they were young?

Joy was puzzled as to why most of the victims she heard about, who had given evidence at the Royal commission, were male. Are there a disproportionate number of boys who suffered in institutions, are the stories from boys what the media most liked reporting or are there still many women who, for whatever reason, have not come forward?

Joy had been following the Royal Commission with mixed interest. She knows a couple whose nephew killed himself after he had been abused by a teacher at a private school. Joy's son Marc boarded at a near-by church school at about the same time and the two schools debated and played sport against each other. She mentioned the lad to her son and was disturbed by his response. "Mum, I can't believe that the teachers didn't know about that teacher! When we were going to sport or debates at that school, the older boys warned us to look out for him."

That had been over twenty years ago and some of those in authority, who should have known better, are still pleading ignorance on the subject.

Joy's thoughts went back to what she had just seen on the TV. At least the men who heard the priest give his evidence to the Commission had got some sort of satisfaction from seeing him put through the questioning. "What of all the others, how are they coping through all this?" she wondered.

Her mind never gave her peace for long and it was only a few seconds before another voice in her head cut in, circling back to what she had just been thinking. "For goodness sake get over it! The guy on TV isn't in any way responsible for what happened to you or the many others you have known and heard about. If he doesn't care about the ones that were in some way his responsibility, what makes you think he would ever care about your lot and the damage they incurred? No one seems to care about that!"

BEGINNINGS

"Be kind. Everyone you meet is fighting a hard battle." Socrates

Errol and Mary, Joy's parents, met on a blind date when he was on leave from the Air Force. They were in their mid- to late-twenties, and they had only known each other for a few weeks before they married. For a while after their wedding, they had moved house every few months. Errol's training for war service was undertaken in several places in two different states. Sometimes Mary went with him and some of the time she remained at home. Joy, their second child, was born when Errol away and he first saw her when she was three months old. His squadron had three hours in the city where she lived before they embarked for the islands north west of Australia. Always hanging over the family were thoughts that he might be killed as many of their friends and relations had been.

For the first years of Joy's life, her father was an absent shadowy figure. He was in Darwin during some of the bombings, before going to Sumatra and Borneo. He was then with the first squadron of the RAAF to enter Japan after the dropping of the bombs, and that had been a traumatising experience for all concerned. One can only imagine how he, like most in the services, would have been anticipating his discharge and return to home and some sense of normality after the war.

War time must also have been an uncertain time for her mother as for most women. Mary, Annie, their first born, and Joy moved in with aunts and cousins whose families were in a similar situation to her own, to her Grandma's house. It was attached to one of the fruit and vegetable shops that her maternal grandmother and uncles had. The women took over the work, often heavy, that the men had done before they enlisted.

When her father returned home after being discharged, Joy was two-and-a-half and Annie was four; possibly the worst ages for children to have a stranger enter their lives. Neither welcomed him with open arms. Joy was angry with him for disrupting the life they had settled into and hit out at him. Annie, being quite timid, was afraid of him and shrank from him. Mary was intolerant of some aspects of his behaviour which were diagnosed some fifty years later as Post Traumatic Stress Disorder. It is likely that he felt disappointed and frustrated by the behaviour of all of them.

Understandably, many couples had difficulty adjusting to life after the war. It is not surprising that Mary and Errol had both changed by the time he returned. The different experiences that they had both undergone in the several years they had been apart made sure of this and meant that there would need to be a time of adjustment and getting to know one another again.

Errol had to train for new work. He had been a commercial fisherman before the war and was also a licensed pilot. Because of his lack of formal education he was unacceptable as a pilot in the Air Force but had spent some time during the war training pilots. Mary refused to let him return to either of these occupations. She saw them both as too dangerous. The best man from their wedding was a pilot and he had been killed in a landing accident. She had already endured several years of thinking that Errol could be killed at any time and she didn't want to go on living with the fear that she would be left with the children if he had an accident or drowned. Fortunately the government offered funding for re-education of those who had served so that was the option he took and he became a cabinet maker specialising in shop-fitting.

When another daughter, Maureen, was born a year later, Mary had suffered back troubles, a carry-over from lifting heavy sacks of potatoes and crates of fruit while working in the shop and these got worse with the pregnancy. She spent as much time as she could lying flat on her bed and out of work hours Errol did much of the caring for Maureen.

Two more girls, Dianne and Lyn, were born, one on Joy's sixth birthday and the last just before her eighth. Annie and Joy took in turns to look after the little ones after school and to cook the evening meals and do the dishes. On Sunday mornings they were rostered to make cake for the packed lunches for the week and to cook the Sunday evening meal. Annie didn't like cooking and so she arranged for Joy to do her cooking and she would do the clearing up and dishes afterwards.

Joy had been an active baby who walked early and at eighteen months had been able to recite poems and hold conversations. She started kindergarten at two because Annie was too timid to go by herself and they needed the numbers to open a new facility. They walked the five hundred metres to and from kindergarten by themselves, taking a long detour on one occasion to avoid the terrifyingly noisy steam roller that was being used to make the road at the end of their street.

There were two things that Joy was particularly fond of from an early age; one was classical music. In the corner of their sitting-room sat an imposing cabinet radio that was usually set to a station that played popular music but whenever she thought that her mother might not be able to hear, Joy would turn its knobs until she found some classical music. It infuriated Mary who would yell, "Get that ghastly chamber music off!"

The other thing Joy loved was flowers. Mary had several small vases and Joy liked picking flowers to put in these. Again Mary complained, "You pick them and I am the one who has to clean up the mess they make."

The family didn't own a car until Joy was fifteen. They rode bikes everywhere. Joy got her first bike when she was four and had soon ridden many kilometres. Once after Annie had started at the school nearly two kilometres away, she left her lunch at home. Mary sent Joy, still a pre-schooler, with the food. The journey was uneventful except that when Joy arrived at the school, she was afraid to enter the yard to give it to Annie. Luckily a teacher noticed her standing at the gate with her bike and asked her what she wanted so that the delivery was made safely. It is impossible to think of a present day parent entrusting such a task to a child of that age.

When she was six, Joy and Errol cycled twelve kilometres each way to visit Errol's father who was sick and staying with his brother. Joy's leg ached for several days after that trip but she was proud that she had made it. She could do tricks on the bike, riding 'no hands' and going downhill with her feet on the handlebars steering were favourite ones. Somehow, she never broke a bone and quickly recovered from the bruises and scrapes that she often had.

PRIMARY YEARS

"My friend ... care for your psyche ... know yourself, for once we know ourselves, we may learn to care for ourselves." Socrates.

Mary and Errol had rules and were strict in enforcing them. Manners, punctuality and obedience ruled supreme. Joy had an enthusiam for life and an inquisitive nature which always seemed to lead her into trouble. Some would have described her as reckless; often remarks were made about her unladylike behaviour and she was called a 'tomboy'. She loved climbing trees and felt restricted by the frilly dresses she often had to wear. Mary was a keen sewer and kept her daughters beautifully dressed. People said, "It's a pity Joy doesn't appreciate the time and effort Mary puts into making her dresses, with the smocking and tatting trims."

Joy did appreciate looking nice. It was just that she seemed incapable of caring for the dresses and aprons that frequently got torn. When eventually there were five daughters and before the days of non-iron fabrics, Mary washed and blued and starched and dampened and ironed and mended up to forty-two dresses on the Mondays and Tuesdays of each week in summer. During school holidays Annie and Joy helped with these tasks.

Perhaps it wasn't surprising that Mary could not spend much time with her children or enjoy their company. She was probably exhausted just keeping up with the household chores. Anyway, she was not the type to cuddle and fuss over her children except for her fourth daughter, Dianne, who was a sickly baby and somehow captured her mother's heart.

They also had strict rules about eating everything that was served on the plate. "I don't want you back here in half an hour whining, 'I'm hungry'! Stay there until you are finished or go down to the fowl house!" Although the fowl house at the bottom of the garden could be a foul place if it was wet or hadn't been cleaned out for a while, Joy found it something of a refuge. She was out of sight there. It was certainly better than getting the strap, cane or the backhanders that rained on her most mealtimes. Sometimes she wore long socks to school, although they weren't uniform, to hide the bruising on her legs from beatings.

But Joy didn't often have to go there for not eating everything. Probably the only good thing about her was that she seemed to get eating right. There was little food that she had trouble with. Once she had commented to her husband, Paul, about a family member who was very thin and a picky eater, and whose mother Joy thought was too lenient on her, "We always had to eat everything on our plate!" "Yes," he said disdainfully, "And look at you now!"

Joy had withered in shame; shame that she had made the comment and shame at her obesity. She had been a heavy baby and an old neighbour had told her, "You were always a chubby little thing, even when you first came to live here," She had been two at the time they had moved to that house. Sometimes adults called it 'puppy fat' and said she would lose it in adolescence, but she never had.

At family mealtimes, she sat at the table immediately opposite her father within easy reach so he could give her "a clip around the ears" when she "deserved one", when her manners were not good or she said or did anything that annoyed him. For years Joy wondered why she was such a slow learner in the matters that were so important to her parents. Why couldn't she behave as they wanted and expected her to? They wouldn't have to hit her so often if she could learn to do and be what they wanted. She meant to be good but somehow didn't turn out to be. She wasn't deliberately bad but had trouble getting her jobs done because she was easily distracted from the task. She often fought with or teased her younger sisters who seemed to have an easier time and get away with things she was punished for.

It wasn't only at home that she got into trouble. At school Joy was often in trouble for talking in class or for fiddling with the pens, pencils and rulers on her desk. She fidgeted; 'ants in her pants' was how Auntie Phil described her constant movement. She loved singing and was ·devastated when she was excluded from a major inter-school choral event because the choir mistress thought she would not be able to sit still on the stage ever though she pleaded to be given a chance.

At the age of nine, when there were three younger children, Joy was sent to live with her grandmother for six months because, as one of her cousins told her with glee, "Your parents can't cope with you." She loved Grandma who still worked more than full time in the fruit and vegetable shop attached to her house and Joy was pleased to go to stay with her except that she had an outdoor toilet which Joy was expected to use during the night. The thought of going outside alone, in the dark, terrified her and more than once she wet the bed rather than venture the considerable distance out. However, Joy's time away didn't do much to improve things with her immediate family and when she returned home relationships were as they had always been, if not worse.

At primary school, Joy usually came in the top eight in her class of fifty five students. She was a whiz at arithmetic, getting her work finished well before anyone else in the class. On a couple of occasions she corrected the work of her teachers that had been done on the board. [That hadn't gone down very well!] And most years she was given jobs to do during arithmetic classes to keep her occupied after she had finished her sums, while the others did their work.

But her reading, spelling, hand-writing and creative writing were dismal. They had few books at home and reading was seen as a waste of time. If her father caught her reading he would roar at her, "Put that book down and get outside or help your mother!"

Joy was clumsy and uncoordinated which led to the humiliation of being among the last one selected for sporting teams. Another of her faults was that she was hard on shoes. Although she tried not to, Joy scuffed her shoes when she walked and from about ten had to re-sole and heel them herself.

Also about that age, her maternal grandfather, Raymond, said to her, "I don't know what is to become of you girls. One of your grandfathers was an alcoholic and the other a no-hoper," referring to himself. He had not held a job for over a week until he was fifty-five when he became a groundsman for a large factory. It had a beautiful garden and he enjoyed working there. Both of her grandfathers were charming to those outside of their family and difficult with those within. Errol's father had been a publican who was reputed to have 'drunk the profits'.

Joy loved climbing trees which was usually a solitary exercise for her. They were a refuge, a hiding place. There was a big mulberry tree in their garden. She had to put on her bathers to climb into it as the fruit juice stained her other clothes but washed from the fabric of her bathers. Armed with large containers to fill with the delicious fruit for her mother to make into jam, she would excitedly climb the branches in the expectation of what she would find there. Of course she had her fill of the fruit as she picked. That was part of the joy of it. There was always an abundance of fruit.

Then there was the apricot tree behind the shed in the back yard of the house opposite where her friend lived. They could only climb that tree when there was no fruit on it so that they didn't squash the fruit, but that didn't worry them because they used that tree as a ladder to get on to the roof of the small shed where they would lie on the sloping roof watching clouds and birds. Part of the enjoyment of the tree was that although no one on the ground could see them when they were up there and they could see all the way to the sea fifteen kilometres away.

At her Grandma's house there was the old fig tree with branches that spread from just above the ground. Joy could climb into its cool branches on a hot day with a book and she would not be bother for hours. She felt safe and peaceful in trees. Perhaps trees acted like cubbyhouses for her and when she was in them she could imagine another life without the troubles she normally encountered.

Because Joy couldn't be trusted enough to look after a "proper school case" when she needed a new one at ten, Errol made her one from wood. It brought her more humiliation. She was teased mercilessly for it and for her home-made blazer. Joy had felt from early on that she wasn't wanted by her parents but she was uncertain as to whether this was because she was different from what they wanted or expected or whether she was different because she wasn't wanted, but these things ensured that she was seen as different by her sisters and her peers also.

Unlike most of the others at school, Joy and her sisters always had home-made clothes with the material often being supplied by Mary's mother. Years later she was surprised to find that a couple of her sisters shared the dread she had of wearing home-made clothes. The husband of one of them said that they should have been proud to have been different after all that was what the Hippy craze was all about, choosing to be different. They all pounced on him at once. "That's the thing," they said in unison. "We couldn't *choose* to be different we were *made* to be different and then made to feel guilty for not appreciating all that our parents did for us that the parents of our friends weren't doing for them!"

Joy started using a treadle sewing machine when she was five and graduated to an electric machine when she was six. She had made her first dress just before she turned ten and not long after was told that as she now could do it, she would have to make her own clothes or go without until she could afford to buy what she wanted herself.

At eleven she won a prize in the under eighteen dressmaking section of the Royal Show. While this pleased her mother, Joy felt that it made her more of a freak at school. Part of the prize was advanced sewing lessons that were held on a Saturday morning. It meant that to attend these classes Joy had to give up her tennis matches that she loved. Mary specially bought a pattern and material for these classes that would challenge Joy's ability and then was critical of the teacher for failing to utilise these things in the way that Mary hoped she would.

In Grade Six Joy clashed with the teacher as never before. The teacher was over seventy and had been drafted in because of the shortage of staff to cope with the post war surge of children that have recently been labelled "Baby Boomers". Joy's presence in the room seemed to annoy Miss MacDonald and she delighted in humiliating Joy by sending her outside or back to a Grade Three class room when she stumbled with her spelling or reading.

This must have been irritating for the Year Three teacher who apparently tired of this because when Joy dropped her scissors on the floor in a craft class Miss MacDonald sent her home. Although she was scared of what her mother would say, there was a naivety about Joy. It did not occur to her to hide somewhere until it was the normal time to go home. She just went straight home to face whatever further punishment was in store. Mary said she must have done something to have deserved such drastic punishment but in an unexpectedly humane gesture, refrained from adding to the punishment because Joy was only one week out of hospital from having her appendix removed.

For some reason Joy never discovered, Miss MacDonald's behaviour changed after this. She wrote a letter of apology to Joy's mother, [Joy was only told about this letter fifty years later]. She never again sent her from the room and Miss MacDonald was content from then on with making snide remarks about Joy's lack of ability.

Every Friday they had a morning of tests on the work they had done that week in arithmetic, spelling and reading. Then in the afternoon, they changed seats in the classroom according to the marks they had received in the tests with the top student going to the far back corner, the second next to her across the back row and working forward. Joy often made it to the back row but one memorable day, she got top marks.

Her joy knew no bounds until Miss MacDonald brought her back to earth with a thud. "You won't last there long!" she said as Joy headed for the top seat. Joy's heart sank. She knew only too well that the moment she did something that annoyed the teacher she would be back in the front row under the teacher's desk. Joy knew that Miss MacDonald would make a big point of how disruptive it was for the whole class to have to be moved mid-week and all because Joy could not sit still. To her delight, Joy managed to stay there for the whole week until the next Friday.

SECONDARY SCHOOL

"Beware the barrenness of a busy life." Socrates

Joy and her sisters were not allowed to bring friends home from school or have them over on the weekends. Whenever they asked Mary's stock reply was a curt, "I have enough to do looking after you lot without looking after other people's children as well." Nor were they allowed to go to the pictures on Saturdays as many of their friends did. "We don't have the money to spend on such frivolous activity. Only people with no imagination have to see films to amuse themselves. It is unhealthy to spend the time sitting inside when you could be outside playing." Occasionally they were allowed to go to the birthday party of a friend.

There never seemed to be enough money for any sort of luxury. Most of her friends' families had cars but they couldn't afford one. Their home and its furnishings were similar to those of the neighbours. Joy didn't think that her dad earned much less than the other fathers at school. He didn't smoke and only bought an occasional lottery ticket. His big indulgence was a vegemite glass of sherry each evening and beer on Anzac Day. Maybe Mary was just extremely careful, frugal or sometimes even mean. Errol worked overtime and did jobs from home as well and Mary did dressmaking for other people. When Joy went to do her Thrift Badge for Guides, the Leader said that she would have to think up something special for her as her family already practiced all the suggestions of thrift in the handbook," Joy was uncertain whether to be proud or ashamed of this.

One of the jobs Errol did at home was to make long rolls of sand paper into circular belts for a joinery factory. This required the paper to be cut into six metre strips and then the ends of each piece were glued together. The measuring and cutting had to be very accurate.

The younger girls could not manage the weight of the rolls and so it fell on Annie and Joy to do most of the work. One girl would kneel at one end of the concrete path that ran across the back of their house, at the beginning of the required length. She would hold the paper on the mark for measuring while the other unrolled the sandpaper in a strip to where Errol would cut the end. Then the roll had to be carried to the beginning again and the process repeated again and again. The sand paper came in different grades and some was very coarse and rough on their hands. They hated this job and dreaded coming home from school to see a pile of rolls on the veranda waiting for their attention.

Annie was a year head of Joy at school and, with the exception of one year, had the same teachers that Joy had a year later. Joy was frequently compared with her. "Annie is such a good girl." "Annie sits still." "Annie knows how to spell these words." "Annie is good at sport." This was another area in which Joy fell short of the expected standard. She had always been clumsy. Things just seemed to slip from her fingers. "Don't let her carry the supper! It will end up upside down on the footpath." "Don't let her touch the good crockery. She's likely to break it" were cries she heard all too often.

Joy was at school in the days of pens, inkwells and blotters. The ink landed in blobs on her work when she was trying hard to be neat. Her nibs got crossed and she just couldn't seem to get the flow of her writing across the page. The letters wouldn't stay on the line. It was frustrating and puzzling that she could be good at needlework and hopeless at this. They were the same hands she was using. Why wouldn't they work equally well in this?

Perhaps it wasn't surprising then that when Annie went to High School it was suggested that Joy go to a Technical School. Joy jumped at the idea of being free from living in Annie's shadow. On the second day of Secondary Schooling, all the new students did I.Q. tests to stream the pupils. Joy was put into class 1S because she had chosen to do the 'general' course rather than the 'commercial' one. She hoped to be a nurse when she left school and at that stage it only required one to have satisfactorily completed two years of secondary education to be accepted for training.

The subjects she studied were English, General Science, Arithmetic, Art, Dressmaking and Domestic Arts, later adding Millinery, Mothercraft and Physiology, just the sort of ideal requirements for any girl expected to be a wife and mother ahead of all else.

Joy longed to be acceptable to her peers. She had given up the idea that she could be liked by others, but if they would tolerate her without humiliating her she could be happy. This was becoming even more important in adolescence. But again her father made a wooden sewing case for her to take to school. Added to this because she was well advanced in dressmaking, her mother insisted that she be allowed to make her own summer school uniform in class. The other girls were making potholders and pencil cases. Again it put her off-side with the teacher who had to prepare different work for her, and the other girls who thought that she was showing off.

Joy wanted to go to a church youth group to which some of her friends went but her parents would not hear of it. Although she pleaded with them a number of times over several years, she was forced to go to Guides. She was not allowed to play netball in winter with her friends as that was the time the Guides went camping. She did quite well there, eventually becoming a Queen's Guide but she would rather have been with her school friends.

Mary sent her children to help people who were less well off. In school holidays they helped at the local Meals on Wheels Kitchen and also at the annual Crippled Children's Camp. For some time when she was about twelve, Joy went every Saturday morning to the home of a local family whose mother was in a Sanatorium with tuberculosis to cook and clean. A couple of years later she went on Saturday afternoons to a home for children with severe disabilities to help feed them and take them for walks.

Joy's most consistent memory of her teens is of her parents arguing. Her mother treated Errol like dirt in front of the children but only argued with him after they were in bed. Then it would start; the yelling and angry words. She could never quite make out what they were saying but the tone was enough. Joy would lie in her bed thinking that if they hated each other so much why on earth didn't they get a divorce? How could they sleep in the same bed after such rows? Strangely she found this more disturbing than much of the trouble she had experienced.

So often it resulted in Joy thinking that all the trouble in their home was her fault. She had been a naughty child. She was bad although it didn't feel like she was. She apparently didn't listen; had been slow to learn things that mattered to her parents like instant obedience. She knew that; they had told her often enough. If she hadn't kept stepping outside the boundaries they would not have to continually punish her and may have been more able to love her. At school or at home, whatever happened, it was always "her fault." The truth that her parents told her was that she was 'a born trouble-maker' and it was their duty as parents to punish her until she learned to conform to the rules they imposed. How else could she ever become a decent citizen?

Talking with her sisters about the trouble between their parents many years later, they said that they suspected their father had been having an affair at the time and cited convincing evidence about the time he got home from evening meetings and groups that he attended.

At the end of second year at secondary school Joy was still four years too young to start nursing. She had just turned fourteen which made her legally old enough to leave school and, much to her mother's annoyance, one of her teachers frequently told her that she was brainy enough to leave and get a job, that only the dull girls needed get more education. This infuriated Mary who wanted her to stay on at school. Mary valued education. She was more highly educated than Errol. She had stayed studying during the Depression and had School of Mines and Industries qualifications in Tailoring and Dressmaking while Errol had only gone to Grade Seven before starting work at the age of twelve. This was quite common for men of his age especially when they lived in remote places as he had done.

The most consistent comment in Joy's school reports was, "Could do better if she tried." This puzzled and frustrated Joy as she did try most of the time and couldn't understand why the teachers couldn't see this.

One other remark that worried her was when, in Year Eight, her class teacher wrote that she was level-headed. Joy thought that this meant she was a block head and expected that the remark would earn her at least a good backhander when her father saw it.

Errol was very strict about any contact they might have with boys. When Joy was about sixteen the church started having dances once a month. Errol embarrassed Annie and Joy by coming to chaperone them. He insisted that they leave to go home on the dot of ten. Later when they were trusted to walk home by themselves, he would hide in the garden to spy on their "Good night" kisses.

Towards the end of Year Eleven which was the year of matriculation at that stage, Joy read about something called Occupational Therapy. She had no idea what it was but thought that it sounded interesting and mentioned it to Mary who became very enthused about this. She found that Joy would have to travel interstate for the study as it could not be studied in the state where they lived. As she had only gone to a Technical School, she would have to have special tests to see if she was capable of the study needed.

It was before the days of standard adult entry tests for Tertiary education and so Joy was assessed as an individual. The Psychologist attached to the Education Department, who did the test was amazed at her results. He said that her intelligence score was well above the level required to study medicine and the results in the maths area were such that she could easily have been a professor of mathematics if she had gone to a high school instead of a Tech. He said that this had all been apparent in the tests she had done on the second day at secondary school and he saw it as neglect bordering on criminal that she hadn't been told this and that it had not been suggested, at that stage, that she transfer to a high school.

While Joy was very pleased with what he had to say and never again doubted her intelligence, it raised questions for her. Why hadn't someone pointed out these results earlier and given her a chance to excel in this way? Had her parents been told and chosen not to do anything about it? It is possible that when her mother had come to the school to see the dressmaking teacher, someone could have told her about the results of those tests giving her a chance to allow Joy to transfer to a high school. She would not have had to go to the same high school as Annie. A new high school had started in their area and Joy could have gone there as her sister Lyn later did.

Was nothing done about her results because in that era, it was still expected that girls, especially ones whose fathers were tradesmen, should be basically prepared for marriage and nothing else really mattered? Could it have been because people from their social class didn't get university educations? Annie went to Teachers' College to become a Primary Teacher.

Mrs Williams, who lived next door, had been disgusted when she heard of the aspirations of a boy from a family in the neighbourhood, "Young Bobby Brown is going to study medicine and his father only sells vegetables from the back of a van. He doesn't even have a shop! What makes him think that he is good enough to be a doctor?"

Joy repeated Year Eleven so that she was a year older before she started tertiary study; however, she was still third from youngest in her year and in many ways quite immature.

TRETIARY YEARS

"An unexamined life is not worth living" Socrates

Travelling interstate presented Joy with a new set of difficulties in being acceptable. Although the Principal of the Occupational Therapy School had warned that it was at least twenty-five percent harder for those living away from home, Joy had an extra handicap. She struggled because she had never learned to study. She had never had to apply herself to pass the subjects she had done at the Technical School and now didn't know how or where to begin.

She was not of the same social class as her fellow students, all of whom had gone to private schools. They were daughters and granddaughters of prominent businessmen and eminent doctors. One told her that she had had a cheek applying to do the course because she came from such an obviously different social class.

During her first year of studying Occupational Therapy, Joy had a placement at a Psychiatric Hospital. Two things happened that had a lasting effect on her. The first was when she was asked to accompany a group of women back to their wing from the activities centre. She was given a bunch of large, heavy keys. The women were waiting in silence at the door. When she unlocked it they wordlessly shuffled across the courtyard to a large gate. Joy unlocked this and it creaked ominously as she swung it open. The women moved *en masse* through the gate and, while she was locking that, moved to the locked door into the building that was their home and placidly waited again for her to unlock this door.

As Joy retraced her steps to the gate, having locked the door again after them, she was overcome with the significance of what she had just done. She felt sick as she wondered what right she had to be locking up fellow humans. "I am only seventeen years old! They are all older than me, some of them considerably so and some of them have been here for years! Surely this is inhumane treatment. Is it really necessary to keep them locked up like this?"

The second thing happened a few days later. A patient kindly asked Joy if she would like a cup of tea and Joy had accepted it and began to drink it. As she did so, she glanced up. Through the large window into the office she could see several staff members roaring with laughter as they gestured to her not to drink the tea. "We *never* eat or drink anything the patients offer us. They do their own washing up and their cleanliness leaves a lot to be desired." The offer of the cuppa had seemed to Joy a kind and generous human gesture and she reasoned that surely it was polite to accept, even if just to give a small semblance of normality to these women's lives. The ill effects that she had from this were from the laughter of the staff and not from the tea.

She was relieved to hear a few years later that the government was closing these large institutions however not enough funding was given to replace them with the care needed for these people to live in the community and many ended up in prison.

Early in the second year of her study, news came that Annie was pregnant and would be getting married on the first Saturday of Joy's next holidays, only a couple of weeks away. Joy felt a mixture of delight and fear for Annie. Joy liked her boyfriend but knew it would have been absolutely terrifying for Annie to tell her parents of her predicament. When Joy arrived home she found that Mary was very distressed and was told that she had been crying ever since she heard.

It seemed to Joy that all of her female relations took her aside at some time during the next few days to ensure that she appreciated just how much shame Annie's actions had brought on the family and how at all costs she, Joy, should "Never also do this to her parents". Joy knew that they were thinking that if such frightful thing could happen to a good girl like Annie, how much more likely was it for Joy to end up the same way. Joy felt quite traumatised by this and immediately broke off her relationship with her boyfriend. They reconnected a year later, but it affected their friendship until she was safely married several years later.

During the time she was studying, Joy did babysitting to augment her income. They were invited to attend classes to learn to care for children with disabilities as the parents of these children often found it hard to leave them with untrained care. The lecturer asked them to imagine that they were having a baby, thinking of their hopes and expectations for the child. Then they were asked to imagine what it would be like after the birth, to be told that the child has a disability which means that they will never be able to achieve those things that you dreamt for them.

It gave them some understanding of the grief and anxiety that such parents live with and the adjustments they must come to. It still bothers Joy when she hears expectant parents say that things like that they don't care if it is a boy or a girl so long as it is okay.

Joy was granted a cadetship to pay for her study and she was bound to work for the Government for three years after she had graduated. Although she enjoyed parts of the work, she often felt lost and unsupported, mostly working alone in a situation where in interstate hospitals there would have been several more senior people working with her. Joy was relieved when the three years were up and she could escape work to get married.

But it was out of the frying pan into the fire in some ways. Although she had known Paul for over seven years, theirs had only ever been a long distance romance as they lived several hundred kilometres apart and only ever saw each other for a day or two once a month. When she had told her mother that they were going to get married Mary had asked her, "Do you love him or have you just got used to him?" Joy hastened to reassure her mother that of course she loved him and it wasn't until ten years later that she realised she had no idea what love was.

MARRIAGE

"By all means marry; if you get a good wife you will be happy; if you get a bad one, you will become a philosopher." Socrates

Married life was not at all like Joy had expected. It was a totally new experience for her; much different from her expectations. She had left her city life to become a farmer's wife. Her paternal grandparents had lived in a remote area and she had visited farms several times as a child but that was quite different to living continuously on a farm. She had to give up her career as the nearest hospital that employed an Occupational Therapist was a hundred and fifty kilometres away. She had to rely on Paul financially and he was even more frugal than she was.

She left her family and friends three hundred and fifty km away, and had to give up tennis which was the only sport she had ever played and through which she had met Paul when he had been staying with his cousin who was a friend of Joy's friend. He was a good player and first in the "A" grade team while she was only "B" grade. The club where he played didn't have a "B" team. Anyway she wouldn't be able to get to the matches. They only had one car and the grades played at different places spread over more than one hundred kilometres so it was too hard to organise.

One Saturday night, a couple of weeks after their honeymoon Joy was feeling quite tired so she went to bed around 8:30. Sometime later an incredible noise woke her from a sound sleep. She sprang out of bed and raced to the lounge room where Paul was looking out of the uncurtained window. There were at least twenty cars in the paddock, lined up all around the house with their lights shining in the as yet uncurtained windows, their horns blaring. Some people were making their way towards the house beating large saucepans like drums. Terrified, she looked to Paul for reassurance. He had not yet come to bed and was still in the clothes he had worn that day. He just stood there laughing at her for being so shocked as people streamed into their unfurnished and uncarpeted living room. She had only met two of them before. The rest were total strangers to her. It was a "Tin Kettling", something she had never heard of.

Noise continued as they put on records, chattered loudly and generally took over her house to organise supper. Joy cowered in her dressing gown in the corner until Paul suggested that she might like to go and get herself dressed. He was cross with her reaction, having not realised that she had no idea what was going on. She was cross with him, suspecting that he had known this was likely to happen but not having thought to warn her. Joy had nightmares about it for some time after. It was for her, another lesson in the differing customs of cultures that had begun when she lived interstate.

It had been necessary for a new house to be built to give them somewhere to live. Joy had expected to have some say in this but quickly found out that the house would belong to the farm and not to her. She had no say in it with all decisions being made by her mother-in-law who had never had the opportunity to build a house for herself before, and Paul. To save money it was decided that the family would paint it and this was not completed for fifteen years until they were hosting a party for Paul's parents' fortieth wedding anniversary. Several times Joy offered to paint the walls but Paul didn't believe women could do the job well enough. As teenagers, Joy and Annie had been allowed to paint the room when what had been the sitting room became their bedroom and it hurt that Paul didn't trust her to do this.

The farm was run in conjunction with her father-in-law and her husband's brother both of whom stayed with them at times as work required. Joy was told in no uncertain terms that woman's work was inside. She would only get in the way if she tried to help, they said. To be truthful, she had no idea about the day to day running of the farm and it wasn't till after the dissolution of the family partnership eighteen years later that she was asked to help with things such as moving flocks of sheep and inoculating lambs.

They were lucky that electricity had been brought to the area the year in which the house was being built, 1967. People living south of them did not get it for another five years. When they married, the farm house could only be reached by going across country for several kilometres through a neighbour's paddocks and scrub. After about two years, a dirt road was formed about a kilometre from the house. When this was bituminised about five years later, it was like they had won the lottery and when another couple of years later they got a phone it was like all her Christmases had come at once. Television reception was always poor; the better the weather, the worse the reception, as they were too far from a repeater station.

Joy's birthday the first year was on a Sunday and when they got to church Paul's younger sister ran to her saying, "We have a chook for you for your birthday lunch."

"That's nice," Joy told her, thinking of the smell of roast chicken. She was astounded to find that the chicken was still alive and that she was expected to kill it. In her family Errol had killed, plucked and cleaned the chooks. When Joy said that she had no idea how to do it, her mother-in-law, who did it in that family, sneered at her saying, "I thought that you would have learned that in Girl Guides!" As a concession Paul did kill it for her but she had to do the rest with the aid of a Country Woman's Cook Book.

Joy felt that she was low on Paul's priorities. The farm and his family came first. He saw his father and brother every day of the week; and his mother was there as well sometimes during the week and at tennis and football on Saturdays and church on Sundays. His football came next in priority and somewhere after that she fitted in. Not that she blamed him. She wasn't much of a catch. They had told her when she was studying Occupational Therapy that she had a depressive personality and looking back, she thinks that she probably suffered from Post Natal Depression although it wasn't until years later that she heard this term.

Joy's first child, Andrew, had a rough beginning. His birth had been long and difficult, three weeks late, labour lasting over three days and ending with a forceps delivery under general anaesthetic. They were both exhausted. She was in a high dependency ward for two days while he was in a humid crib even though he had been a healthy eight pound twelve ounces. Twenty-four hours after his birth a nurse wheeled the crib to the foot of her bed and said, "This is your son." Joy has vague memories of looking and seeing very little except the bruises and swelling caused by the forceps and of him being taken away again after a short time.

Andrew was the first grandchild and he a boy. What more could a farming family wish for? At least Joy had managed to get this right! Joy was in a room immediately opposite the nursery where all the babies were kept in those days. There was a large window into the corridor and the babies were placed near the window for relatives to see. Sometime during the evening Joy became aware of the voices of her parents-in-law in conversation with another farming couple, friends of theirs, whose son and daughter-in-law had also had a son. Both couples were delighted with the new babies and were saying how beautiful they were. In Joy's eyes, new born babies are rarely beautiful for the first couple of weeks. They are incredible beings, but beautiful was not a word she would use especially for Andrew with the bruises and swelling from the trauma of his birth.

On and on both couples went, saying that the babies had this person's eyes and that one's nose etc. "How can you tell with the swelling?" Joy wanted to call out. Beauty was certainly in the eye of the beholder and she was relieved that Andrew's looks greatly improved over the next couple of weeks. She was astounded to hear some time later that the other baby had Down's Syndrome. The doctor had recognised this at birth but believed that the parents should get to love him as a normal child before being told of his condition. While Joy understood this reasoning in light of the excited chatter she had overheard, she thought that she would want to have been told immediately if it had been her child.

Andrew was about six months old when, having been in to town, Joy stopped at a friend's place on her way home. They were having a cup of tea when the friend's husband burst in saying, "Dad's just shot himself. I'm going to get Fred" [his brother who lived next door]. He turned and ran from the room.

Joy and her friend sat stunned, looking at each other for a few seconds and then her friend said, "He must be injured. I'll hold Andrew while you go to see." She grabbed Andrew from Joy's arms. Reluctantly Joy walked towards the shed where the shooting had taken place. She knew the man. He was ninety-one and a member of their congregation. She found him lying in a pool of blood with a rifle beside him and a wound to his head.

Joy lent down to feel for a pulse in his wrist. She could still feel something but all her first aid training about stopping the blood loss had deserted her. She dropped the man's arm and raced back to the house. He had an appointment with his doctor that afternoon and so Joy rang the doctor. By this time she was trembling so much she could hardly speak. The doctor listened to what she said, said that he would get the ambulance immediately and then said, "You know he can't survive this. He will not last till the ambulance arrives. Prepare yourself for this."

It was reassuring that the doctor came with the ambulance and they arrived at about the same time as her friend's husband and his brother arrived back about half an hour later. The rest of the day is pretty much a blur for Joy except that she had difficulty getting her friend to relinquish Andrew. She wanted to cling to him as if the reality of his existence reassured her in some way that life would go on. From then on Joy has felt that it is important to have children at funerals to give hope that life continues in the middle of death.

About that time there were several severe car crashes with a number of young people killed, some of whom they knew. At one of the funerals, the minister was going on about their loved one being forever with God in a magnificent heaven. It suddenly appalled Joy. Up to that moment, she would have been saying, "Yes, yes," to the minister's words but now she saw them as empty platitudes. Joy decided that it was important to give people something to live for in this life so that they wouldn't take silly, life-threatening risks. She felt it was wrong to tell them how good heaven was going to be without giving them hope that life in the present was worth living.

CHILDREN

"How many things can I do without?" Socrates.

One day, when Andrew was about ten months old, Joy was holding him and said quietly, "I think that I might get to love you sometime." She liked that thought and found it encouraging but it didn't automatically help her to love him.

When he was about eighteen months old, someone commented that he looked far more like her mother-in-law than his mother, his Grandma had said, "Thank Goodness!" Joy bristled, wondering if there was something wrong with her looks or whether Joan had doubted his parentage and therefore her fidelity.

About that time her second child, Jessica, was born. When she was about six months old and very cute, her brother hit the "terrible twos". The grand-parents' allegiance shifted from Andrew to Jess and for some time neglected him to fuss over her. Joy could see his pain and became fiercely protective of him for. This didn't last long as Joy struggled more and more with life.

Joy cannot remember when she began yelling at Andrew and hitting him. She thinks that it might have started as an attempt to get Paul's attention. He was hardly ever home but in a catch twenty-two situation, her behaviour when he was there was such that he didn't want to stay. She was always tired and spent a lot of time crying. When Andrew was about three, she read in a magazine a plea from a mother who said that she was physically abusing her child and was worried that she might kill him. Joy thought, "I could have written that letter." The mother was advised to go to an organisation in the city in which she lived for help.

But Joy lived hundreds of kilometres from a city and felt the situation was hopeless for her.

Paul rarely gave her presents which irritated Joy and added to her feeling that she didn't matter to him. However, she understood why he behaved like this when she heard her mother-in-law's attitude to receiving gifts.

A group of women were at the home of a neighbour for a meeting. One was admiring some of the home owner's ornaments. The woman said that her husband quite often came home with a gift for her. Joy's mother-in-law commented. "If my husband did that I'd tell him to take it straight back to where he had got it from!"

Paul didn't tell Joy what he was planning and so if she didn't ask she was left unprepared for when shearing was starting or whether she would have extra workmen for lunch some days. She learned to keep her pantry and freezer well stocked for such occasions. After they got the phone, Paul would ring his mother in the evenings and Joy would learn what was going on by listening as he told Joan. He coached football fifty kilometres from their home on Tuesday and Thursday evenings and was away all day Saturday. Joy and the children went with him to football most weeks and helped in the canteen and on the social committee which was expected of the football wives, but when he went to tennis in summer, she and the children just stayed home. It was as easy to look after them at home as at the matches so she might as well stay home.

For the first few years there were only two families within a ten kilometre radius of their farm and one of those was fifteen kilometres away by road. The one place they went together every week was church and she always looked forward to the contact with other people that that provided.

In spite of how wretched Joy felt a lot of the time, they always presented as a happy couple in public. She frequently cried herself to sleep at night. She knew she wasn't a good wife or mother and was a disappointment to Paul, certainly not what he had expected. From time to time, he repeated an accusation first made on the third night of their honey-moon, "You had other boy-friends besides me."

She repeated her reply, "Well of course I did, just like you had other girl- friends." He had kept the letters that four girls had written to him when he was wool classing in station country. Joy realised what he was on about many years later, well after Paul's death, when she heard of the practice of people from Pacific Islands. The young couple had to bring the sheets from the marital bed to church the morning after the wedding where older women would examine them for blood to prove that the bride had been a virgin. There had been no blood on Joy's sheets and Paul had held that against her all those years.

Paul, like her father, didn't call Joy by her name. A woman who was new to the district tried to find out Joy's name by asking Andrew, "What does your dad call your mum?" "Wife," was his reply and much to Joy's consternation, the woman thought the story amusing enough to repeat it several times. For weeks, friends and neighbours told Joy, "She told us about asking Andrew what your name was," and would laugh at the joke. But it wasn't a joke for Joy. She tried to rationalise that it was reassuring that Paul claimed her as his but in truth, it felt as though she was an object, a possession instead of a person.

Joy had married Paul because she trusted him. He didn't try to force himself on her before they married which was a relief given what happened to Annie. It didn't occur to her that this was because he wasn't much interested in that side of things. From early on, they only made love when she initiated it. While this had felt safe to begin with, it soon became frustrating. Still, it was no use complaining. Her mother's words came back to haunt her. "You made your bed. You lie in it!"

When Andrew was nine and Jess seven, they had another child. It was a week past her due date and the gynaecologist thought that she might be having twins. Joy wasn't well so it was decided to induce the birth. Just as the doctor came to examine her, the umbilical cord prolapsed. Everything became frantic as the doctors ran with Joy from the labour ward to the operating theatre and the birth was competed by C Section in four minutes. Paul said that the nurses cried as the baby cried.

The next day Joy thanked the doctor for saving Marcus. Tears trickled down the doctor's face. "Do you know what it is like for us when we fail to save the babies?" he asked. Then, after a pause, he added, "Were you praying?"

"Yes," Joy replied.

"I knew it!" he exclaimed. Then this Hindu man went on to tell Joy how he had been going back to his rooms after lunch. In the car-park he suddenly had the feeling that something was going wrong at the hospital. He yelled to a colleague who was getting out of his car to come to the hospital with him and so the two of them arrived just in time.

On another visit, the doctor said that it worried him that so many Australians dismissed the idea of praying. "It helps us when you pray," he said.

Now Joy was constantly tired and disorganised and it was Jess who did much of the caring for Marc in the first few years. Joy managed to get some housework done by dividing it into small blocks. She would put a record on the radiogram and work until that record finished and then take a break. She aimed to keep the garden in some sort of order by weeding a square metre a day and envied those she heard say that they had spent the afternoon in the garden.

A woman had told her that she had had trouble with Marc's birth because she was so fat and at a supper, a man handing around a plate of food had come to the person sitting on her left and offered it to her. Then he stepped back away from Joy and back again to offer it to the woman on her right. As he did so, he said to Joy, "You don't need this. You're heavy enough." Such comments caused her much anguish.

LOVE

"Living well and beautifully and justly are all one thing." Socrates.

In her musings one day a couple of years later, Joy realised that she did not feel any love Paul or the children. She felt guilty and ashamed and that it should have been apparent to her before this. She did look after them reasonably well and did much that was expected of a farmer's wife in those times from feeding shearers to working to support all the local groups, schools and hospitals but she did it because it was what you did rather than because she loved them.

"Love," she thought, "is supposed to be a feeling but when I look at my family, I feel nothing. I don't even know what love is!" Love, in her mind had been too confused with corporal punishment; tough love they called it when they hit her. Joy heard at Sunday School of God being Love, and of loving God with all our hearts, minds, souls and strength. She had been told that there were five different forms of love in the Greek in which the Bible had originally been written. She could only remember three of these; Filial that was brotherly love [she wondered if sisterly love came into it], Eros which was sexual love, and Agape which was the pure love of God. Where did loving your neighbour as your-self fit into this, she wondered?

Joy began to ask others what they though love was and it soon became clear that very few people had ever tried to put it into words. Some said love was caring. But, working in Community Health, Joy had seen plenty of people who cared from a sense of duty and didn't love. Because of this, Joy recognised that she was quite good at saying what was *not* love. She could pick up on that almost instantly!

Although Joy was generally seen as a friendly person, she had few close friends. She just couldn't risk people getting close enough to find out how bad she was. She was a fraud. In the community she was seen as diligent worker, contributing to a number of organisations but at home she failed miserably, especially when there was no one to see and increasingly there were only the children as Paul kept out of her way as much as possible.

A couple of months before Marc turned five, Joy found out that the acne from which she had suffered for years was caused by a hormone imbalance. Joy had never self-harmed by cutting herself as some disturbed people do, but since her early teens she had picked at her face, arms legs and body. She would attack any spot, freckle or blemish with vigour to dig it out. It had started when she had her first boil at the age of twelve on her left knee. A neighbour had commented at the time. "Once you've had one boil, you will have them for seven years." Joy had endured them for thirteen years before they stopped as suddenly as they had started. By then she had many scars. The boils had stopped but still she picked at her skin.

People implied that both boils and acne were caused by uncleanliness. Every now and then someone would remark about a cleanser or method of washing that they thought Joy might find helpful. One suggested she try "Solvol" and another, a particular brand of dishwashing liquid. She accidentally swallowed some of this and had trouble breathing for several minutes. Joy went to a local medical clinic to have a blood test that was required before seeing the dermatologist. Her usual doctor was away so she saw a different one. She had spoken to several doctors during the years about how tired and depressed she felt and had been told such things as, "This is usual for a mother of young children," or "If you lost some weight you'd feel better." She had tried various weight watchers groups five times but without dramatic effect. It was depressing in and of itself to be always reminded of her weight. This time the doctor had said to her after taking the blood, "Well that was quick. Is there anything else I can do for you while you are here?"

It was June and Joy was miserably cold so she replied abruptly, "Not unless you can make me warm. I'm always cold."

He sat looking at her for a few moments and then said, "I think we'll get the blood tested for thyroid function as well.

The doctor rang to tell her the results and said, "If you are travelling over three hundred kilometres to see a specialist, you can make the trip more worthwhile by seeing two."

When Joy saw the skin specialist, he said she may have irreparably damaged her skin trying so hard to clean it when lack of cleanliness was not the problem.

On the same day Joy also went to an endocrinologist as the tests had shown that she did have an under-active thyroid gland.

The symptoms of hypothyroidism for her went back more than twenty five years. When Joy was about the age of ten, Mary had bought boots for her to wear to school because she complained of being cold. They were an embarrassment because boots were out of fashion. Mary used thick lining on Joy's coats while her sisters' coats were lined with beautiful satin. She was tired, depressed and overweight as well.

When she started on the medication for both conditions, the changes in her life were dramatic. Joy was no longer tired, cold or depressed and had much more energy. It was remarkable. She no longer put on weight but to her disappointment, neither did she lose it.

NEW LIFE

"The secret of change is to focus all your energy, not on fighting the old but on building the new." Socrates.

Looking back and using an analogy from her profession, Joy is unsure whether her rehabilitation began the day she started on thyroid replacement therapy or whether it had started when she decided to find out about love, but start it had. She hadn't set out to find herself but this was, in the end, what it was all about. During her questioning about love, it became apparent to her that she needed to allow herself to be loved to learn what love was. It was like she had built walls around her to stop anyone getting close so that she couldn't be hurt and in doing so had cut herself off from love. She consciously made an attempt to be less defensive with others.

She began to get on better with Paul and had become more patient with her children. She still had low self- esteem and almost no confidence. A group of her friends were going the fifty kilometres to town to attend Penguins Club meetings for developing their skills in public speaking. Several times one or other of them tried to get her to come along with them but Joy just said, "It would be a waste of time. You will never get me standing up in front of people speaking!" She volunteered to be treasurer of a couple of organisations because the treasurer did not need to even sit up the front.

At the beginning of 1984 Joy started a two-year full-time pre-vocational course in Fibre Craft at the TAFE College fifty kilometres from her home. It was in the town where Andrew and Jess were at

Secondary School. Marc had just begun school in the small town eleven kilometres from home. For some years Joy had been spinning and knitting woollen garments for sale and she was also a member of the local Embroiderers' Guild but had realised that her work needed to be more saleable if she was to make much money from it. She had done some weaving at school and wanted to try that again too.

It was a rare treat to have the course offered at a rural campus and Joy didn't want to miss out on the opportunity. However, there was a difficulty about doing the course. The students had to pass the design and drawing component before they could proceed with the craft aspect. Joy was a competent craftsperson but fear of this requirement nearly defeated her.

In the middle of her year eight, the Art teacher called her mother to the school and said that Joy was so hopeless at art that it was a waste of time her even completing the year and that she was being swapped out of the class. The trauma of this humiliation was still with her in her late thirties when she wanted to do this Pre-vocational Craft Course.

By this time Paul had retired from playing football although he still coached the Colts team. He was a great encourager from the coaching, and now constantly told Joy, "Don't let it beat you! You can do it". It also improved her relationship with Andrew and Jess as they watched her struggle with homework as they were doing. She was delighted in the second year when a visiting lecturer from the capital city art college told her that she had a drawing talent and he would be happy to have her in his class if she ever came to the city to live.

Joy found it useful to hang on to the idea of the lecturer who taught them to make improvements by practicing something small over and over and endeavouring to do better each time. She said that it was like learning to play a musical instrument and encouraged them to be pleased to learn thing better in small steps and not to expect to be perfect the first time.

Joy did not pass the course brilliantly but she did pass and her self -confidence had started to rise from rock bottom where it had been for many years.

It had been a hectic two years to get the course completed and she decided to take the next year catching up on housework and family things before launching into Fibre Craft professionally. Towards the end of the year she received a call from a Health Centre forty kilometres away in the other direction from where she had done the course. They had received funding to employ an Occupational Therapist one day a week and would she be interested in the position?

Joy wasn't very enthusiastic but they said that it would be almost impossible for them to fill the position outside of the district. No one would relocate to such an isolated place for a one day a week job. So although this had not been in her plan and she wasn't sure that her new found confidence extended to this, with Paul's encouragement she decided to give it a go. There would be time on the other days of the week for her to do her fibre work. Even so it took her a while to decide to go ahead with it. She needed to organise to do a refresher course and began this in January of the following year, 1987.

For this Joy would have to go to the city three hundred kilometres away each Monday and come back home on Friday. She stayed with her parents during the week. She was shocked at how little she knew of new understandings and methods that had been developed in Occupational Therapy since she last worked and felt quite inadequate when she started at the Health Centre. She began work hoping that she would be able to continue to catch up and keep up with new developments, a big ask in the mid-eighties before anything was available on line.

Paul, who had banned her from working off farm early in their marriage said jokingly after a few months, "You are so much more interesting now you are working. I wish I had sent you back to work years ago!" It had expanded her horizons again as she met more people and became part of a new community.

As Joy and Paul approached the end of the second decade of their marriage, things had started to improve between them. His parents had retired, the farm had been divided between the family and responsibility handed over to the next generation. Paul was free to make his own decisions about the future direction of the farm. Sport was taking less of his time and he was more reliant on Joy for help with the livestock.

One day about this time, Paul came home from a Bible Study and said, "I had never realised that the passage from Genesis says, 'A man shall leave his father and mother and cling to his wife.' I have always assumed it was the other way round; that the woman should leave her family and I see now that I have never left my parents for you."

Joy had become aware of this several years earlier at a spinning group when the women had been talking about the difficulties of marrying a farmer. Almost without exception, the women present had left their homes and families and moved on to the farms of their husband's families. They probably had their own home, but the family business was so much the core of their husband's life that the women all felt like strangers who didn't fit and weren't encouraged to fit in. There is a saying that you have to be born in a district to belong to it and with farming families it often seemed that you needed to be born into them as well.

Paul pledged to do his best to make her a priority in his life and this was another step forward in their relationship. In February 1988, just before their twentieth wedding anniversary, they went to a marriage enrichment weekend which was good and Joy was full of hope for the future.

Andrew had finished year twelve and was now working part time on their farm and part time for others in the district.

They talked of taking a trip overseas next year when Andrew knew a bit more about running the farm. He was doing an "On Farm Training Course" an apprenticeship for young farmers, and was also working at home. Jess was in her final year at school and would be at university next year. Marc was in year 5 and doing well. Joy was feeling hopeful for the first time since she was a child.

ABUSE

"Sometimes you put up walls not to keep people out but to see who cares enough to break them down." Socrates

A few months after she had re-entered the work force, in her early forties, Joy went to a meeting of the Parents and Friends Association at the Secondary School her older children attended. That month the guest speaker was a Social Worker whose clients were mainly victims of sexual abuse. Joy was interested in what she would have to say. It was the first time that she had heard anyone talking about the topic and it had an unexpected impact on her life.

When the speaker at the Parents and Friends Meeting asked for questions, the woman sitting next to Joy stood and announced to the whole room in what seemed to Joy like an unnecessarily loud voice, "I am a victim. My father abused me." The words exploded from her like an erupting volcano. There was a stunned silence as people came to grips with this.

As she sat down a tiny vent opened in Joy and she whispered to the woman, "My father abused me, too". It was the first time she had ever said those words and she felt quite shocked and vulnerable at hearing the admission. It was a relief as well, though. Some pressure had been released inside her but at the same time saying the words aloud had forced her to start thinking more realistically about thoughts she had from time to time.

One of Joy's memories was when she was about seven years of age. Her father worked in a dusty factory and had a shower each evening when he got home from work, before tea. Annie was old enough to shower herself but it was usual for Joy, Maureen and Dianne to be bathed at the same time as Errol showered to save water. The shower was over the bath as was often the way things were back then, with a plastic shower curtain to prevent the whole room getting wet. The three girls sat playing in the bath while their father washed himself and then he lifted Joy up to him.

She put her legs around his waist as children do and then he tried to push her down lower on his body. She squirmed and he got impatient with her.

"I thought you liked it," he said.

"Well I don't!" she had protested and then asked, "Why does it go like that?" pointing to his erect penis.

Her father laughed and said the hot water made it happen. He still held her but didn't try to touch her with it again.

Not long after that, Joy's mother had said to her, "I think you are old enough to have your own shower now." Joy had been pleased to be granted this bit of independence.

Contemplating the memory as an adult, Joy had wondered at the words in the memory. Try as she might she could not remember her father having held her like this before, but if he hadn't, why did he say, "I thought you liked it?" And why had she been so emphatic in her reply, "Well I don't!" It was like she had determined that she had had enough and wasn't going to put up with it any more.

The other memory that bothered her possibly happened about the same time. It was usual on the weekends for them all to pile into their parents bed when they woke in the morning. Joy remembered this as a special time that she enjoyed. But one day she was late getting there. She had needed to go to the toilet and her younger sisters had got there first. There was laughter and other happy noises coming from the room as she hurried up the passage eager not to miss a moment of this precious time when her parents weren't usually cross with her.

As she threw herself at the bed that day, her father hissed, "Not you!" Joy jumped back. She stood at the foot of the bed, looking at him for an explanation of this unexpected behaviour.

"You're too old for this now," he said sharply. But it was not his words that hurt her most. It was the look of disdain on his face and hatred in his usually blue eyes that seemed strangely black. Joy had never seen anything like it. She slunk from the room to sit in confusion on her own bed before getting dressed and going outside. Joy presumed this was part of the aftermath of her complaint in the shower.

In her adult life, Joy began to wonder if there had been other incidents as well as these two. Several times when her husband had suggested something a bit different in their love life she had reacted with an almost terrified, "Don't do that!" There were other things about her behaviour that puzzled Joy. She couldn't work out why she was almost fanatical about getting up before the children and when they woke, she would call them down to the kitchen to keep them protectively under her wing like an old mother duck. And there seemed to be no reason for the panic that she felt when she found Andrew, then about four, in bed with her husband Paul's elderly aunt.

They were all staying at her in-laws home for a wedding that had taken place the day before and Joy had uncharacteristically slept in. When she went to check on her children, Andrew had called to her as she passed the door of Auntie Elsie's room. She looked in and saw him lying there in Elsie's bed, chatting away as happy as Larry. He had wandered into the room when the rest of the house was still asleep. When Auntie Elsie spoke to him he said that he was cold so she had invited him to jump in with her to warm up and to keep him from disturbing the others.

Joy's first instinct was to rush across the room and grab him out of the bed. Luckily she realised in time how irrational her thinking was. Andrew was okay and not distressed in any way and Elsie was totally trustworthy. Even so it was somewhat reluctantly that she left them and retreated to the kitchen feeling confused. Her anxiety only subsided to a manageable level when, a few minutes later, Andrew came running to her.

There was also the way in which she reacted when her father-in-law teased the children. Sometimes Jim had needed to stay with them to help Paul on the farm. The children, toddlers at the time, were accustomed to running to the bedroom naked after they had had their bath. They adored their Pa and Joy thought very highly of him except for this one thing. If the children heard his voice in the kitchen, they were likely to be diverted from their mission and run into see him. He would shout at them, "Rudie, Rudie!" and pretend to chase them. They would giggle and flee to their room to get their pyjamas on.

On the one hand, Joy could see that it was intended as just a bit of harmless fun. But on the other she was furious with him for, as she saw it, sexualising the innocent nudity of childhood. Why did everything have to be sexualised? It made her feel sick and she wanted to scream, "Stop it!" at him. She knew that her reaction was out of all proportion to the behaviour. She trusted this man as she had never trusted anyone before. Why had he had to say this! Enormous disappointment swept over her. Were no men safe to be with or for children to be with?

Joy was sexually assaulted several other times. Once when she was fourteen, at a football match, she was in a crowd waiting to get a drink at half time when a man behind her put his hand up her skirt and into her nickers. She managed to squirm away from him and get out into the open and back to the safety of her friends. She was shocked and too scared to tell anyone in case they had said it was her fault, that she must have done something to provoke it.

A seemingly small incident, but one that added to her distrust of men, happened when she was about eighteen. A couple from the group of friends that she hung out with offered to drive her home. When they got there, the young man had parked his car in front of the next house down the street. She thought this was a bit odd as there was parking space in front of her house. Then he said that he would walk her to the door which she thought was a kind gesture and she chatted happily as they went.

When they got through the gate and near to the house so that the fence blocked the view from the car where his girl-friend sat, he forced her against the wall and began groping at her clothes, his body pressed tightly against her. She was shocked and felt sick and disillusioned as she raced to get away from him and into her home. What had seemed like a gentlemanly offer must have been a premeditated ambush. Why else had he driven past her house? She has had to face the man many times since then as the couple were good friends of Annie and her husband and she often wondered if he remembered and felt any guilt about his behaviour.

Another time in her late teens, on an overnight train returning home for the holidays from her study interstate, she was in a second class carriage where you sat up all night. Most of the others in the carriage were Naval Cadets. She was wakened when the one who was sitting next to her grabbed her hand and clamped it on to his erect penis. The carriage was in darkness and all of the other passengers seemed to be asleep. Joy didn't scream but may have given a shocked gasp. She had learnt not to make a fuss when her parents were beating her and so could keep quite when others would have yelled out. A frequent threat had been, "You can stop that crying or I'll give you something to really cry about." As soon as she could she levered herself free from the man and terrified, turned her back to him, clasping her hands together to prevent him grabbing one again.

Wide awake, she sat there trembling, thinking that was the end of sleep for her that night. However, not long after, the conductor came up to her and said, "I have found an empty seat, where someone has got off the train. Would you like to come and sit there?" Joy had been unaware that anyone had noticed the man's behaviour and has no idea who the person who saved her from a night of misery was but she was forever grateful.

Another seemingly small incident, but one where she felt decidedly uncomfortable, occurred when she had to undergo a medical examination as a candidate for ministry. They were given a small list of doctors who did the examination and Joy chose to go to the nearest one. She was somewhat surprised that he told her to strip and lie on the table. It had been many years since her doctors had required her to strip. He did not offer her a sheet or blanket for cover. Then standing beside her he scanned her body from toe to head and said with a leer, "What is it like lying naked before a man after several years of widowhood?"

An angry Joy reported this incident to a female lecturer who agreed that his requests for her to undress completely and his comment were inappropriate. To Joy's relief she later heard that the doctor was excluded from the list that future female candidates were given but at the same time she wondered how safe his other patients were.

Joy had often wondered if she is supersensitive in labelling these incidents abusive. They seem so small. They were all over quickly. Probably most people would say, "What is she on about? There was no harm done! Why didn't she just laugh them off?" But how would they know? Each incident led her to trust men less and feel increasingly angry towards some of them.

The Social Worker had invited anyone who would like to, to ring her after the meeting to make an appointment to see her. Joy desperately wanted to do this but there were all sorts of implications in admitting to herself that what had gone on in her childhood *had been* abuse. She had never told Paul and was quite certain that she could not now do so. Paul had such strict morals. Errol was still alive. How was she going to face him; and Mary? What was her mother's role and responsibility in what had happened?

DILEMMAS

"An unconsidered life is not worth living." Socrates.

One of the dilemmas for Joy was that in more recent years, for some illogical reason, she had blamed her mother more than her father for what went on in her life as a child that contributed to the problems she had with relationships as an adult. Her mother was diligent in feeding them, keeping them well clothed and forming them into responsible citizens but was emotionally detached and had never hugged them. The only "love" Joy had known was this abusive stuff from her father who was continually ridiculed by her mother. She almost felt sorry for him and was inclined to forgive him.

It took Joy nearly a fortnight to pluck up the courage to make the phone call. When she did, the Social Worker said to her, "There were fifteen women at that meeting and you are the ninth one to get in touch to say that you were abused. We have decided to get together next week to have a chat. Would you like to come?" Joy had no idea just how life-changing her decision to go to that meeting would be.

Not all of those who had spoken to the Social Worker came to the meeting, but most of those who did decided to keep meeting once a month for coffee and a chat. All had been astounded at the number from the original meeting who had admitted to being abused. One commented that there may well have been one or two other victims who simply could not or did not, for whatever reason, make contact.

For most it was good to be talking about this thing that had blighted their lives, this thing that they had kept secret because of the shame. As adults most had persuaded themselves that they were at least partly to blame. Often this view was aided by some of the things that had been said to them by their abuser. Most also had not heard of any other victims and had thought that they were the only person that it had happened to. This was in the late eighties when such things were rarely spoken of. Some of the abuse that the others had suffered was considerably more violent than what Joy had experienced. For some it had been a "one off" event, but for most it went on for months or years. None, in adulthood, had confronted their abuser.

The Social Worker recommended that they read several books, one of which was available from the local library about a woman who had been similarly abused. Joy borrowed the book. It was an easy read and she was able to identify with much the woman had to say. One thing really bothered her though. When the woman had told her husband about the abuse, he had become very angry with her for 'deceiving' him; blaming her and, seeing her as polluted, he refused to touch her for over a year. Joy could not bear the thought of enduring that but she thought it quite likely that Paul could respond in a similarly angry way.

The woman's husband had a couple of questions and a statement that were to come up over and over in the years ahead as Joy spent more time talking about this issue. The first was the accusatory comment. "You must have known it was wrong!" The implication of this is that you, the victim, a child or vulnerable adult, should have told someone or done something to stop it. Joy thought this statement raised more deep questions about the nature of knowing right from wrong; is it instinctive or learned and if it is learned, how and at what age? One of the techniques used by sexual abusers is to swear the child to secrecy either by offering a reward if they don't tell or threatening harm if they did.

Joy has thought long and hard about whether she was somehow to blame for this abuse. As indicated earlier, she had decided that she didn't like what Errol was doing but at no stage did she think of it as wrong. She now believes that for many things, children need to be taught what is right and what is wrong and she hadn't been taught that this was wrong. For her it was a normal part of life.

Some of the others, who had been older when the abuse occurred, did recognise that it was wrong but for a variety of reasons didn't or couldn't tell. Some were persuade to silence with bribes, others with threats.

It was unrealistic to expect children or even vulnerable adults where there was a distinct power imbalance between those involved to tell back then. It was a different time before "No means No" campaigns and when it was unacceptable to speak of things sexual. You need to have some realisation that this behaviour is not acceptable to even begin to contemplate who to talk to about it. When it is normal behaviour in your home, you think that it is normal for others, too. How can you be expected to report it to someone else? Then if you learn it is wrong, the shame of coming from a deviant family is likely to silence you.

Some who came to the meeting just wanted to go home and forget about the abuse or learn to live with the reality of their lives. But along with several others at the second meeting the Social Worker held, Joy was enthusiastic in wanting to help others now they had found support for themselves. One woman worked for the local health service while Joy, by now, was employed by the health service ninety kilometres away. They both decided to speak to doctors and other workers about the support group and ask them to consider mentioning it to anyone who talked to them about abuse.

They got a mixed reaction from this. Some professionals were supportive while others were openly hostile. Joy's boss was relieved that such a group had been set up. She had an immediate recommendation. A woman in her sixties, with several brothers and sisters, had just spoken to her about the abuse she had suffered at the hands of her father. Her parents were both in their eighties and when the woman had finally said something, they both denied the abuse and all her siblings had turned against her. The trauma of this rejection had been almost too great for the woman to bear and she was grateful to find someone who took her allegations seriously.

The response of this woman's family further convinced Joy that she could not say anything to anyone in her family. She couldn't bring herself to ask her sisters directly so she left the library book, and another one the subject that she had purchased, very obviously on the coffee table when her sister, Dianne, came to stay. She casually dropped into conversations with Annie, Lyn and her mother that she was working with adult survivors of childhood sexual abuse. She had scrutinised them carefully as she had said these things, but no one showed any reaction, asked any questions or seemed the least bit interested.

Not surprisingly, perhaps, Joy decided that it must have only been herself who had been abused in the family. She certainly hoped that had been the case.

Annie had once said when they had been talking about something else, "You remember so much more of our childhood than I do."

Some months later, Joy had read that when you can't recall your childhood it could be because it was too painful to remember. She photocopied the page and sent it to Annie who later told her that she realised that this was probably true.

Several years earlier, when Joy and Annie had been talking about their childhoods, Annie said to her, "You know you weren't responsible for our parents not being able to cope with you as a child. Look at your own children. Would you hold them responsible?"

Joy agreed that indeed she would not blame her primary school aged children. She hadn't realised how seriously she had taken the idea that she was to blame for all the trouble. For several days, every time she remembered Annie's words she cried with relief.

A couple of years after the meeting with the Social Worker, when she was visiting, her mother said suddenly, "Your father was a very passionate man; passionate in every way."

Joy was perplexed. "What is she on about?" she wondered, but said nothing. Nor did her mother add anything further. On reflecting later Joy thought. "Was trying to tell me that she knew what went on?" Joy didn't know what to do about this. She didn't know how to bring it up directly with Mary. For a while, she mulled it over and then she got angry.

When her mother had stopped her showering with her father, had she also stopped his behaviour or had he just moved on to her younger sisters? Did he prefer younger girls as indicated when he stopped her getting into bed with them and the younger ones?

On the other hand though, it seemed reasonable to Joy that she had been the only one. She was the "black sheep" of the family. She was the only one who seemed to find it impossible to do what she was told. She didn't mean to be naughty but for one reason or another, she was frequently being caned by her father or strapped by her mother. Her father had once said that he was going to hit her till her nose bled. Imagine both his and Joy's surprise when the first time he struck her, blood spurted from her nose. It stopped him from hitting her any more that time - but it was not long before he thought that she needed to be punished again.

Joy was sure that both her parents hated her except for the times when her father was fondling her. They told her often enough that she was more trouble than the rest of them put together.

Joy continued to meet with the other victims. About half had been abused by their fathers or step-fathers, others by neighbours or other relatives, grandfathers or uncles. While Joy was pleased to have found people who understood aspects of her life that she had long thought unspeakable, a terrible secret and shame, she was becoming increasingly worried about how to continue to keep her involvement in the group from Paul. Of equal concern was how she could tell him and how he might take it.

There were a number of reasons why she could not bring herself to tell Paul and neither could she bring herself to say anything to her parents. It was impossible for her to visualise how a conversation would go. When she spent more than a few minutes in their company, Joy reverted to her adolescent fear of them.

The price of "coming out" might be too high. Also, Errol was still alive and what if her parents and all her sisters turned against her as that other family had done? She was not brave enough.

At the family Christmas Dinner that year there were five granddaughters under the age of eight. Joy spent the day keeping a close eye on her father and the little girls. She had read of a time when a perpetrator had managed to abuse a girl while in the same room as her parents without anyone suspecting. They could be very devious and she had no doubt that Errol was a smooth operator.

In a paradoxical way, Joy would need to feel angry to make the accusation but she realised that it would not be wise to do it when she *was* angry. She had learned from her aunt and her father that they had a tough upbringing. When Joy had married and gone to live a distance from him, she got on much better with him. Joy didn't feel any closer to her mother but still lived in hope that one day their relationship would improve so she just let things continue, hoping that something would occur that would make it possible for her to tell Paul before he heard something about her association with other survivors on the grapevine that works so well in rural areas.

DECISIONS

"We cannot live better than seeking to become better." Socrates

For some reason, Joy was seen as the "religious one" in the family though Annie must have come a close second. She was given a Bible for Christmas the year she finished grade three. Annie had been given a prayer book by her God-mother and Joy always envied her for it. Joy had made several attempts to start at the beginning and read through the Bible but was later to learn that this is a particularly difficult thing to do. When she was in her early teens, Annie told her that it was about time she started reading the Bible every day and provided her with a guide for this.

The teacher Joy had in Sunday School in her early primary years, had been a missionary in China. Her stories were incredibly exciting to the seven and eight year old. This was what she was going to be when she grew up. Then somewhere in her late Primary years she read "The Nun's Story", and decided that she was going to be a nun. A couple of years later someone explained to her that she was the wrong denomination to be a nun and that she would have to be a deaconess. This is what she then set her sights on. When instead, she studied Occupational Therapy, Joy rationalised that she could become a medical missionary. Then two things happened to change this. She met Paul and then found out that her home state had less Occupational Therapists per head of the population than large parts of India. So she stayed home and married Paul instead.

Joy continued reading her Bible daily, taught Sunday School, attended Bible Studies regularly and worked for trading tables and other fund-raising ventures for the Church. Both Paul and Joy were teetotallers and that alienated them from many in the district and especially the football club with its culture of heavy drinking. Paul seemed to largely take this in his stride but Joy could be quite self-righteous and judgemental about those who didn't meet her standards.

As the years passed, Joy became less and less satisfied with the Bible Studies they were doing. There was no room in them for individual thinking or questioning. The writers of the studies left room for only one answer to their questions and Joy was increasingly sure that often there was more than one way of looking at some of these things.

In the mid nineteen eighties, the congregations went through a Pentecostal phase. They did "Life in the Spirit" courses and they prayed to be baptised in the Spirit. Most spoke in tongues but Joy never did. This led to a number of others saying things like that she wasn't praying hard enough or that she didn't have enough faith, even that she wasn't baptised in the Spirit. Joy was puzzled why she didn't receive this gift because she had judged herself to be every bit as devout as the others. And when she prayed earnestly and still couldn't do it, she was more than a bit cross.

Paul couldn't see what the fuss was all about and preferred his religion the way it had always been, simple and straightforward. He surprised Joy when he said after a men's group, that they others had been talking about God speaking to them and that he had never heard God speak to him. Joy said nothing to him, but prayed that Paul would hear God speak to him about the future of the farm.

Now that Andrew had left school, there was not enough work for both of them full time and so several possibilities were mooted. They could buy more land. There were several lots for sale near their place that each had things going for them. Or they could redevelop what they already owned. They would have to borrow money to buy and Joy didn't like that option. She preferred not to go further into debt.

About a month later, Paul was rostered to do devotions for the Elders' meeting. The next morning, he told Joy that he had heard God speak through the reading he had used for the devotions. They would go ahead and buy a particular block of land. Joy was so startled by this that she didn't ask Paul any details about the experience, something she would live to regret. She did think though, that if they were to buy anything, that block was the best option.

They had to borrow all the money to pay for it as was common practice among farming folk at the time. Advisors from the Agricultural Department and Bank agreed with the proposal but there were delays in finalising the sale. During this time, interest rates on the money they had organised to borrow began to rise.

One afternoon Paul was going to show his mother around the new farm and asked Joy if she would like to go too as she had not yet seen it. She was busy at the time and they were going in the ute so it would not be comfortable with a third person in the front seat, so she declined the offer. "Next week, after settlement day, you can take me. We will go to every corner of the place and you can tell me what you plan to do with it," she said.

Paul told her that he had inquired about insurance for the new land. "For three hundred and five dollars, we can get insurance to cover the whole cost if anything goes wrong," he said.

"You will get the insurance?" Joy asked.

"Oh yes," Paul replied, "but we don't need it until settlement day," which was 20th July.

A couple with whom they had been friends for many years had been asking them for some time to go on a houseboat holiday. Joy had been reluctant but had finally agreed. In the July school holidays, Paul, Marc and Joy had three days with their friends on the Murray River. It was a wonderfully relaxing time during which Paul celebrated his forty-fifth birthday.

Joy was sorry that she had limited the time, wishing that they had had at least a week. "Next time we'll make it longer," she thought.

DEATH

"True wisdom comes to each of us when we realise how little we understand about life, ourselves and the world around us." Socrates.

The issue of telling Paul about the abuse however, became the least of her worries when, five days later, he died suddenly. Joy was about to go to lunch at work when a doctor rang from the town 90 kilometres away where Jess was at school. Joy assumed that he wanted to speak to her about a patient as her area of responsibility overlapped his. Instead she heard him say, "Is there someone with you?" When she answered, "Yes," he went on, "Your husband has had a heart attack and we have failed to revive him."

There was a moment's pause as Joy digested this and then she said, "You mean he is dead."

"Yes," the doctor replied.

"I don't know what to do," Joy said, floundering to make sense of this news. [She had learnt as an Occupational Therapist that people can say irrational things when they are in shock.] "Should I go home?"

"No," said the doctor. "Come here. Andrew is here alone."

Joy was to learn later that Andrew had been trying to drive Paul to hospital but he died well before they got there. They had been out in a back paddock, at least five gates from the road and six from the house. Paul told Andrew not to stop to ring an ambulance but he eventually did stop at a farm house close to the road. There was only a very deaf, elderly man at home and it took Andrew a while to convince him he was in trouble. To begin with there was no way the man was going to let an agitated teenager into his home to use the phone.

Afterwards the man walked back to the car with Andrew. He took one look at Paul and said, "He's dead, mate!"

Andrew had replied, "Yes, I know, but I have to keep going!"

He had met the ambulance only a kilometre from the hospital.

When she heard that Andrew was at the hospital alone Joy snapped into action mode. "Get the minister, he'll know what to do," Joy told the doctor, "It will take me about an hour to get there."

The woman who was with Joy, Judy, had been widowed ten years earlier at thirty-one when her husband was killed in a car accident, leaving her with two boys aged nine and eight. She was a great help to Joy over the coming months, in part because her sons had been the same age as Marc now was, when their father died.

Joy's boss wanted one of the other workers to drive Joy to the town but Joy wanted to drive herself as she would need her car. If they went in her car, someone else would have to go to bring the other woman back. Eventually it was decided that they would let Joy drive her car with Judy following to make sure she was alright. The chemicals released into her body by the shock of the news meant Joy was on a sort of high, and felt slightly numb.

By the time Joy arrived at the hospital, the minister had assembled her mother-in- law, Joan, and her best friend, Beth, to be with Andrew. Joy was met on the steps of the hospital by a youngish police officer who was in tears. "I played tennis against Paul recently," he said and then went on, "You don't have to identify him. Andrew has already done that."

"Good heavens! Is he old enough?" Joy asked.

"Yes, I checked he was eighteen," he said. But Joy was thinking more of the burden on a lad of eighteen being asked to do such a thing. There was more to this as Joy learned later that because Andrew had been with Paul when he died, he had to be questioned by the police to establish that he had not contributed to Paul's death. Six weeks later, after the coroner's inquest, Andrew received a letter clearing him of any responsibility for Paul's death.

Joy went with the minister who had also been a friend of Paul's to see his body which they had placed in an empty room at the hospital. The day before had been National Bible Sunday and the minister had asked them what their favourite Bible verse was.

Joy had said, "Ephesians 5:20, "Give thanks to God for all things." Now in a sarcastic voice she asked, "Is this what God means about giving thanks for *all* things? Am I supposed to give thanks for *this*?"

The Bible verse Andrew had said was, "All things work together for good for those who love God." He said later that the words had gone round and round in his head all that day and then when Paul had doubled over in pain and said, "Get me to hospital," the words had flooded back and stayed with him even though he realised that Paul had died.

The verse kept Andrew going and Joy thought that somehow God had known Paul was going to die and had given them this gift to encourage them through it. When she mentioned this a woman had said, "Well, of course God knew he was going to die. The Bible says that our days are numbered from birth." Many people hold this belief, sometimes in its secular form saying things like, "His number came up." In spite of what had happened, Joy is unsure if she believes this is what happens.

The minister, Grandma and Beth took Andrew back to Grandma's house while Joy went to the High School to pick up Jess and tell her the terrible news. Paul's father had died just three years before following open-heart surgery, at sixty six and so Joan was very upset at now also losing her older and favourite son.

How do you tell a child that their dad has just died? Nothing in life prepares you for such a duty. Joy wanted to use the word dead so that Jess, and in turn, Marc, were not left having to try to work out what she was telling them as she had been with the doctor. "There's no easy way to break such news," she would say later. "Even if it takes you ten minutes of beating round the bush, the result is the same when realisation hits."

Joy arranged for a neighbour to bring Marc from his school forty kilometres away to Joan's home. She rang her mother to tell her, and her sister, Maureen, answered saying that Mary was out shopping but would be home in ten minutes. She would get her to ring back.

The local funeral director was soon there to begin to make arrangements. He was a good friend of Paul's brother, Peter, and their families had spent the Sunday afternoon together. Peter had asked the funeral director how business was going and he said that he had had a very quiet month. "What I could do with is three quick deaths," he said. The first phone call he had received was for Paul. The man was devastated. As he talked with Joy about the funeral arrangements, he kept saying, "I am so sorry about what I said," as if he thought his words had caused Paul's death.

Joy waited six hours for her mother to ring, saying several times, "I wonder when mum will ring," and later, "I can't go home till mum has rung. I don't want to miss her."

Finally around nine pm, Joan persuaded Joy to take her children home to bed and they made their way to the farm three quarters of an hour away. When they left, Joan immediately rang Mary. "Why haven't you rung? Joy has been worried," she said.

"I was waiting till she knew the funeral arrangements. Tell her I'll be there about an hour before the funeral," was all Mary said.

Joy's parents were both retired. Although she hadn't realised it, she had been hoping that they would come straight away to be with her. Her sister Dianne had been planning to leave on a trip around Australia with her family and they had left their home as soon as they finished packing the caravan so that they arrived at the farm just as Joy and the children got home. That was the kind of support that she was hoping in vain for from her parents.

Paul had been the fittest man in the district. Joy was forty three and their children were eighteen, seventeen and nine years old. His death was devastating with the family losing not only the man, husband, father, son, brother, income earner, companion, encourager but eventually losing their home as well. But in all that was one relief. She would never have to tell him about her father.

Joy tried at one stage, to tell her minister, but he stopped her. "You cannot talk to me about this. You must find someone else if you need to talk," and he walked away leaving her feeling unclean and let down again.

"The least he could have done was to suggest who that someone else might be!" she thought.

Little in life prepares a person for the premature death of their partner. There are no lessons at school about how it feels or what to do. Joy had read the book, "Good Grief" and so had some idea of the stages of grief but she was under the mistaken view that it would all be over in three months or so. Little did she suspect that it would continue in diminishing waves for the rest of her life!

Back in 1988, when this happened, the idea was to get the funeral over as quickly as possible. Paul died on a Monday morning and the funeral was arranged for the Wednesday afternoon. This did not give much time for coming to terms with his death or for customising the service in any way. Joy quickly learned that it was not "her" funeral. Others wanted their say it what happened and there were protocols to observe. Marc was nine and an excellent reader. He wanted to do a Bible reading in the service but the minister would not hear of this, saying that he might break down. Later Joy regretted not insisting that Marc could do this last thing for his father.

There were issues also about viewing the body. Joy felt that this was important. She could understand that Andrew did not want to go with them but in the end, Paul's sister and her husband and children all went at the same time as Joy, Jess and Marc. Afterwards, Joy wished that she had just gone with her two and let the others have their time alone with him. "It is important to get it how you feel comfortable the first time. You don't get a second chance at these things," she said.

Her mother-in-law, Joan, had said to Joy, "You will find the day of the funeral relatively easy. You seem to get extra strength for it. It is in the months ahead that the real difficulties come." She had been right.

There were an estimated six hundred at the service with footballers from two different clubs forming guards of honour at the cemetery. Many offered help but few were available when Joy needed them. "Sorry, I'm busy today. Can you ask someone else?" seemed to be a common response.

About six weeks after Paul's death, a woman elder came from the church and told Joy that she had a crush on Paul. She went on and on about what a wonderful man Paul had been compared with her husband and how devastated she was by Paul's death. Joy thought her behaviour was quite bizarre and spoke to another elder about it. That one said, "So what if they were having an affair, you can't do anything about it now he's dead." This reply left Joy speechless. For her, a crush on someone and an affair are quite different things. She wondered if the woman knew something she did not and wished she hadn't said anything.

One of the things that people said frequently to Joy after Paul's death was, "You have lost your husband." After several had said this, she found herself saying, "No, I have not lost my husband. I know exactly where he is. He is in plot 474 at the Lawn Cemetery. It is me who is lost. I no longer know who I am. Paul called me 'wife' for twenty years and, especially in more recent times I have tried very hard to be a good wife for him."

Joy had even done a "Philosophy of Christian Womanhood' course about three years before. It emphasised the importance of the man as the head of the house. It taught that it was the man's place to make decisions within the marriage and the woman's to obey. Joy had practiced this for about six months diligently until Paul said he had failed to notice anything different in her behaviour. This disappointed Joy and she relaxed the rules she had for herself a little.

"Now I am no longer his wife. His death has left me feeling that I have had an arm and a leg ripped off." When she said this, another widow in the group added, "And half your heart ripped out as well."

Eventually Joy came up with this analogy. "Marriage," she would say, "Is like two bushes of different varieties being planted in the one hole." She had heard on a gardening show that they suggested growing a climbing rose and a clematis plant together as they complemented each other and neither overpowered the other. "Over time they grow and become more intermingled so that after a while they may look from the distance like a single entity.

When one dies, it is like it is ripped out leaving a hole. The remaining bush is left feeling lopsided, exposed and vulnerable, in danger of toppling. It takes much input from other people over some time, to even partially fill the hole [It can never really be filled], heavy pruning and perhaps even staking before the surviving plant can be sure that it is going to live and may even begin to grow on from the trauma."

"When a father dies, the children are like smaller bushes that have grown up in the shelter of the larger ones and are likewise damaged by the death."

One day about six months after Paul's death, Joy sat down with a pen and a lined sheet of A4 paper and began to write. On every line she put another loss that she and the children had suffered since his death. She had lost her husband and also companion, income earner, her children's father, the person who made sure the car was serviced and filled with petrol, the wood chopper. They had lost friends. She had lost her trust in people when ones who had said they would help were always too busy to come when she asked.

On and on the list went until she had filled the whole page. Then she sat back and took a deep breath. "That is quite some list," she said. "No wonder we all feel so rotten. I could turn the page over and keep going but this is enough to see the extent of our losses."

Most of Joy's energy was taken by the needs of her children, working "off farm", running the farm and then when that failed, eventually leasing it for others to use. About a year after Paul's death, Joy also began working three days a week on one of the first Aged Care Assessment Teams to be set up. She enjoyed it initially when she thought that she would be able to catch up with her knowledge of Occupational Therapy but distance from libraries and other facilities and the extra responsibilities she had with the family and farm made this impossible. Eventually it was clear that she needed to do her degree all over again if she was to continue in this work or she could take the opportunity to study something completely different.

Jess had gone to the capital city to University in the February following Paul's death. Then a couple of years later, Marc had gone to the same city for Secondary Schooling and Andrew was about to start an apprenticeship there too.

It was hard to put up with the comments of well-meaning people who had their own ideas on what had happen and why Paul had died. Some said, "God [or Jesus] has taken him," to which Joy wanted to say, "Well, we wish God hadn't!"

Some said, "Paul's work on earth was finished." Or "God had work for Paul to do in heaven." To these Joy wanted to say, "How do you know? We, especially nine year old Marc, don't think this way."

Some said, "You have been specially chosen to bear this cross," and "God only gives such pain to those who are able to bear it." Sometimes Joy wanted to hit these people. A couple implied that it had been Joy's fault for not looking after him properly. Some even suggested that she should be rejoicing that Paul was now with God forever. Others said that Paul was in heaven looking down at her and caring for her. Joy didn't like that idea at all. It spoke to her of Paul keeping an eye on her. She couldn't get on with her life thinking that she was continuously under surveillance. "If he has to keep an eye out for me, that sounds more like hell than heaven to me."

In the years before Paul's death there had been two occasions in their district where there had been two couples who were good friends and then one of the husbands had died. In both cases, a short time later, the surviving man had left his wife and gone off with the widow. In both cases, the gossip around the district completely blamed and vilified the widow. There was no doubt in the minds of all that it was the widows who had caused the man to leave his wife. Joy vowed, "I will never do such a thing! I could never take another woman's partner from her." In spite of this there were times when she found herself hoping that a woman would die so her husband would become available.

About a year after Paul died, Jim, an Elder from the church who was the husband of her friend June, started making suggestive remarks to Joy. Several times he said things in front of June and she just laughed. This irritated Joy. She would have been cross if Paul had said such things to another woman. She wanted to tell him that if he was the last man on earth she wouldn't want anything to do with him but instead, in her embarrassment, said nothing to him. When he left the room after one such conversation where he had said that June was going away for the weekend and would Joy keep him warm in bed, she said to June, "Will you please ask Jim to stop saying those things."

Again June laughed as she said, "Oh, I trust Jim. You have nothing to worry about."

Joy was now furious with June also and replied perhaps a little too loudly, "Yes, but can you trust me? I don't even know if I can trust myself!"

June looked stunned and Joy was disappointed and cross that in the heat of the moment, she had put herself down to make her point.

However, it worked. Jim didn't ever say anything after that but it had damaged Joy's relationship with June. She felt let down by her and she couldn't understand how a woman could laugh in such a situation. Joy wondered about the couple's relationship that he would behave like this. It seemed insulting to June and Joy began to wonder (again) if any men were trustworthy. She was afraid and felt that she had to be constantly on the alert in case she inadvertently slipped up in her behaviour.

Joy longed for close relationships, but realised in her late forties, that when a new friendship, either male or female, looked promising, she would sabotage it. She was better than she used to be but still whenever someone who she liked moved past a certain incomprehensible point, Joy would do or say something that would cause the person to back off. She could be quite nasty on these occasions and then would become distressed when she realised the consequences of her actions.

About two years after Paul's death, Joy went, with a friend whose son had been killed, to a workshop on grief for people who had lost a significant person in their lives through death. They were given a sheet of brown paper about two metres by one point five metres. They were told to put it on the floor and then they were each given the thickest red felt tipped pen she had ever seen. Then they were invited to write on the paper everything that had been said to them that was NOT helpful.

To begin with, there was stunned silence in the room. Then there was palpable anger as they began remembering and saying out loud and writing. Then there were cries of "Yes, yes!" as they got it down on the paper. The noise in the room grew and developed into cries of laughter as tension was released as those present shared the things they had found unhelpful like, "You'll soon get over it," or "You must forgive." or "You'll get married again; there are plenty more fish in the sea." Or "You can have another child."

There was no doubt that every person present had been frustrated by things that had been said often by well-meaning people who had no idea how much their comments had hurt.

When everyone had finished writing, they were invited to screw the paper into as tight a ball as they could or tear it into shred and also form it into a ball to be kicked or thrown around the room. When they ran out of energy, the balls were consigned to a bin for recycling into cardboard.

The change in atmosphere in the room from before the exercise to after was remarkable. The tension was gone. Joy felt like a huge weight had been lifted from her shoulders.

Over the months, Joy struggled with all the different implications of God's place in their lives and especially in this death that was such a tragedy for them. They were hundreds of thousands of dollars in debt and frugal Joy, whose family had not had a car till she was fifteen because they refused to buy anything they could not pay for in cash, found it very difficult to think that God may have added to her burden by telling Paul to buy this land.

At the time it had seemed a direct answer to her prayer and she had been delighted with the outcome. Could she have been a bit smug? She wished that she had asked Paul more about it. Joy had found out that the text Paul used that night was about Caleb returning from the Promised Land full of hope with enormous bunches of grapes which held great promise and were seen by Caleb as encouragement to go ahead into the land.

There was her apparent instruction to "give thanks for all things" alongside Andrew's "All things work together for good…"

Interest rates on their loans continued to rise to nearly 20% and the price of wool, their main income, dropped significantly.

Paul had died two days before settlement day and subsequently Joy found out that settlement day was only a symbolic day. They had responsibility for the finances and had effectively owned the property from the day the papers were signed two weeks earlier. Paul's good intentions about getting the insurance had amounted to nothing.

Joy discovered six months later that on the morning he died Paul had tried to ring his insurance agent to put a cover note in place to get the insurance that would have covered the cost of the new land. The agent had been out and when he got the message and rang back he was told that Paul had died. The person who answered the phone had no idea why Paul had rung the agent and it was many months before Joy found out about this. She also never found out who had been in her home and answered the phone that afternoon.

Joy sold the new land seven years later when she could no longer bear the burden of the debt. She received only half of what they paid for it and was still paying the bank the difference and the interest on the debt fifteen years later when they sold the remaining land of the farm.

Because Paul had left the farm equally to each of his children, there was no way that any one of them could make enough money from it to buy the others out especially with the change in economic circumstances for wool producers and the recession in Australia. Two years after Paul's death, their assets were valued at one fifth of what they had been when they got the loan for the land.

Joy had noticed about the time that her father-in-law had died, that when women in country areas were widowed, they almost always lost their homes soon after as well. Seventeen men had died in the district since she had been there and only three women. The men had ranged in age from thirty-ish to seventy three. Within a year of their husband's death, only two widows were still living in their home. Most had moved into neighbouring towns. Given that moving home is a grief-promoting event in itself, this added to the suffering and disruption of the women's lives. It "might be best in the long run" but it is added pain at the time.

The other thing that Joy noticed in this was that there was a drastic need for research into men's health to find out why they were dying at this rate. The Community Health Centre ran workshops on women's health but nothing was done for men in those days. Joy was pleased with the gains that had been made for women through women's liberation and now thought it was time for men's liberation to become a priority.

About this time Joy realised that she would need to find full time work. She was still in her early forties and so had many years of working life left. Because she had been a city girl and had been excluded from outside work on the farm she knew little of what was required to make a success of the farm; not that anyone could under the economic circumstances they now had. She contemplated doing a new degree in Occupational Therapy but felt more drawn towards becoming a Deacon in the Church and started making enquiries about this.

It had surprised her how many of her clients in the Health Service wanted to talk about spiritual things, especially if they were facing death or had been very ill. This wasn't in the usual brief for Occupational Therapy even though it covered an enormous range of healing, but it seemed to show an underlying concern for many when they were given a terminal diagnosis. Sometimes they had been associated with a church earlier in their lives but even some agnostics began asking questions when they were faced with their own mortality.

A few weeks later, she felt sure that in her heart she wanted to be a Minister of the Word rather than a deacon. This bothered her because in her head, she was equally sure that women should not be ministers. Women were supposed to be silent in Church. But it seemed that she was being told that there was work for women to do. Joy was worried about what her minister might say. She was also worried that she might be deluding herself and felt very conflicted.

Eventually she plucked up courage to go and tell her minister. He remained poker-faced while she spoke and said he would have to think about it. She retreated, somewhat disappointed with his response, but on her way home felt strangely light as if a huge burden had been lifted from her.

Then after the service a couple of months later, the minister said, "About that matter you brought up; if God is calling you to be a minister of the Word, God would have gifted you with the ability to preach. To prove your commitment to the call, you must do the Lay Preachers' Course and then we will be able to see if you have the gifting." He never spoke to her again about the matter. Joy enrolled to do the course by correspondence. The lectures were sent to her on tape, some video, which was difficult as they didn't have a video player. Joy had to travel a hundred kilometres there and back to her mother-in-law's home to watch them.

From the beginning of Old and New Testament Studies, Joy was almost overwhelmed by what she was learning. It was so different from the Bible studies she had been doing for many years; so much more interesting. The minister left to go to a new placement a couple of years later and by that time, Joy had more work as an Occupational Therapist on an Aged Care Assessment Team. She had convinced herself that this was the way for her; to do this work and be a Lay Preacher and never spoke to anyone about having thought about being a minister.

They had leased the farm but she was living in a cottage on the property. Andrew was about to start an apprenticeship in diesel mechanics in the city where Jess was in the final year of her degree at University. Marc was to board in the city for secondary school because of Joy's work commitments in two different towns ninety kilometres apart. Their farm was too far from either a school or a school bus. He was classified as an isolated child by the government receiving an allowance to help with the cost of boarding.

At the beginning of that year she had taken Marc to start at boarding school. The Headmaster had addressed the parents. "It is a sad thing to leave your child here, hundreds of kilometres from where you live. When you get home there will be an empty bed and that is not easy to see." Joy thought, "When I get home, there will be four empty beds that were all full three years ago!"

A new minister had come in the January and one day in the third week of August, Joy went to his home after work to borrow a book that she needed to read for her final subject for the Lay Preaching certificate. She sat in the kitchen, talking to his wife while he went to his study to get the book and when he came back, he placed it on the table next to her and said, "You can keep it. You will need it when you get to College."

Joy swung around to face him. There was no doubt by the look on his face that he meant what she suspected he was saying. She said slowly and carefully, "I did once think about being a minister. How did you know?"

He replied that the first time he and his wife had met Joy they knew immediately. "We discussed it on the way home and decided that we would wait for you to tell us when the time was right. You could start studying next year. There is a scholarship you could apply for and the applications close at the end of this month. How about you put in an application as a test? If you don't get it you will know the time is not right."

Somewhat dazed, Joy promised to think about it. As she was leaving, the minister's wife gave her a large bunch of flowers she had just picked from her garden. The perfume filled the car as she drove the fifty kilometres to her home. Her mind was going round and round. This was the last thing that she had expected when she stopped by to borrow the book. She had convinced herself that she was to be a lay preacher and now this had come up!

Joy didn't get much sleep in the next few days as she worried about whether it was the right thing to apply for the scholarship. Eventually she decided to go ahead with it. If she got it she would go and if she didn't, nothing would be lost. Several days after she had visited the minister, she was searching in the back of a cupboard for another vase. It seemed that everywhere she had been in the last few days, someone had given her flowers. This continued. When she visited clients in their homes, something she did several times a week, they said things like, "Let me pick a few roses for you before you go," or "The stocks are so lovely this year, would you like some to take with you?" Her house began to look, and smell, like a florist shop.

Joy put in her application for the scholarship and, while she was waiting for the reply, she kept receiving flowers. A fortnight later, she was notified that she had gained a scholarship and could start studying in February of the next year. The next day, she received the last bunch of flowers for that time.

Still, Joy had settled into a routine that she was comfortable with after all the upheaval of the previous three years and now her life could be turning upside down again.

JUSTICE

"The highest realms of thought are impossible to reach without first attaining an understanding of compassion." Socrates

Without realising it, justice had become a passion for Joy. When funding for assistance had been withdrawn by the Education Department for a client of hers with special needs, she had asked the members of her local school Parents and Friends Association to lobby the government for a better deal for all children with handicaps. She was upset when they declined to help and the head teacher had explained that there were no children at this school with a handicap and so the parents just didn't understand. "Or care!" Joy thought.

The Health Centre where Joy worked and in whose district she lived, provided care for people in their homes all over the district, even in remote places. The Health Centre in the district where their church was had a different policy. If people needed help, they were required to move to the big town to receive it which often meant much disruption for the families. One day in late September, as they were having morning tea, Joy suggested that as most of them lived in that district, it would be in their interest to lobby the council to change their policy.

One of the elders flew into a rage, shouting at Joy, "Get out, get out. We do not need trouble-makers like you in our church!"

Stunned, Joy backed out the door with the woman following her all the way to her parked car, poking her finger at her and shouting. Then she said, "There isn't room for both of us at this church. I have a husband who needs to work his farm and you do not have a husband. It is you who must go!" When she talked to the minister he saw this incident as further proof that it was time for Joy to move on. Joy followed his urging and left three months later to study.

No farewell was held for them and about three years later the church closed, was sold and demolished leaving only an empty paddock where Paul had worshipped all his life, having been an Elder, Chairperson of the congregation and Sunday School Teacher. Their children had been baptised there and Jess had chosen to be married there even though she had moved away for study and work because it had been so much part of her life. This was another considerable grief for them.

When Joy told her mother, Mary, that she was going to study to become a minister, her mother wrote her a letter saying that she didn't think that Joy had realised it but she had deliberately set out to stop Joy becoming a Deaconess when she was a teenager and that she was pleased that at last she was having the opportunity to do what she had obviously always been meant to do. This was a stunning disclosure. Joy hadn't realised it but looking back, Mary had been very keen to get her into Occupational Therapy and when she had sometimes been asked why she had done it she had said, "Because my mother wanted me to."

It took her more courage to break the news to her father. Errol was so critical of the Church and of those who had anything to do with it. He was sitting in the family room when Joy approached him. "I am going to study to become a minister," she said and pausing only slightly, she left the room. She didn't know if he had his hearing aids in and if he had heard her. Ten minutes later, Joy was in the kitchen talking to Mary.

Errol came to the door. "Oy!" he said.

Joy looked up. "Yes?" she said cautiously.

"You can bury me!" he said, turning on his heel and walking away. Joy knew she had his approval.

During the time Joy continued to work in the country, she kept in contact with the group of survivors of abuse which was encouraging for her. Occasionally they had other victims join them or one or more of them were asked to meet with a survivor. This term was generally used when the abuse had been many years before and they had managed their lives reasonably well.

NEW BEGINNINGS

"Education is a kindling flame, not the filling of a vessel."
Socrates.

At the beginning of February 1992, Joy moved several hundred kilometres to the city to begin a degree in Theology. It was thirty years to the day since she had begun her previous tertiary education. She did not know at this stage if she would be going on to complete the five years of study and formation required to become a minister. She still thought that this may be some kind of a test from which she would eventually be released so she chose to board at the college instead of finding a house or a flat to live in.

This also meant that Marc was still eligible for Government assistance in boarding, and knowing that he was being taken care of made it easier for Joy to study. His school was only four kilometres from where she was living and so she was able to watch him play sport and debate and he came to her for exit weekends. They went home to the farm for each holiday.

It was about this time that it dawned on Joy that if she thought that something was simple or was going to be easy, she probably hadn't understood the subject or task. To her amusement she later heard that someone had compiled research from around the world that said "the more people thought they knew about a subject, the less they probably did and the more they did actually know the less they thought they did."

To become good ministers, the church encouraged candidates first of all to get to know them-selves and to understand their own needs and behaviour. Joy was told, "If you are aware of your motivations, you are less likely to try to get your needs filled by others which may lead to abuse."

Because of this, as part of the degree, Joy chose to study Psychology 101. It was liberating to learn that some of her behaviour was due to genetics like her personality type as an introvert. In particular, Joy could only stand a certain amount of noise and busyness. She liked to get away after a while from others; to find somewhere peaceful and quiet. When her children were younger, she had got up an hour before anyone else in the house to have some quiet time before the chaos of the day. She had always liked to go to bed early so she would wake in the morning for this time, but that was only part of why she disliked staying long at evening events such as cabarets. The noise nearly drove her to distraction. Then she had felt guilty for spoiling Paul's fun; now she understood why she found such events intolerable.

In Psychology there was a segment on Sects and Cults and brainwashing techniques such as sleep-deprivation, isolation from familiar surroundings, loud music and bright lights. This was disturbing as Joy could see that some activities run by the church, such as the Easter Camps for young people, inadvertently created situations similar to some of the techniques used by cults. Of course they were less of a problem because they only lasted four days but the realisation alerted her even more to the need to examine her thoughts and the motivation for her behaviour.

Another segment was on unquestioning obedience. They were told how, at the War Crime Trials at Nuremberg, many people pleaded that they had killed because they were obeying orders. Experiments were carried out that showed ordinary people were willing to administer lethal doses of electricity to other people because they had been told to do so by people in authority.

Joy had been brought up to unquestioning obedience. Many of the beatings she had endured were because she had trouble in achieving this. Not only that, but she had also understood that God demanded unquestioning obedience. "Trust and Obey for there is no other way to be happy in Jesus" had been taught well to them at Sunday School and in Religious Education. Now she was being taught that unquestioning obedience was a bad thing, that it was not good to want to please others at all costs or to demand that others obey you.

This new idea caused Joy to question whether God required such obedience and whether the Church was right or being manipulative in its teachings. She wondered how much of her interpretation of the Church's teachings had been governed by her parents' demands and punishment. There was freedom in not having to obey and there was also the need to take responsibility for your own decisions and actions, but overall, Joy found this liberating.

An equally challenging experiment that they heard about was conducted at Stanford University. The researchers took some ordinary people and divided them into two groups; one to be guards and the other to be prisoners. Some who had been allocated to be guards behaved so appallingly towards those who had innocently become prisoners that the experiment had to be discontinued before the scheduled time. It seemed that some people, when given authority, immediately became bullies.

In Pastoral Care, they were told, "We not only have to do the right thing but we need to be seen to do the right thing." They learnt about abusive behaviour and that there are a number of different areas in which it is seen in relationships; physical, psychological, emotional, financial, social, religious and sexual.

From her experience, and from what she had heard from other survivors, sexual abuse was almost never isolated from other abuses. Almost always, some of the other forms of abuse, if not most on the list, were present. She had never had a broken bone and her father had never raped her, in the traditional sense of the word, so far as she could remember, but the lecturer had explained that in law, with a child, it does not require full penetration to be called rape.

Joy recognised elements of most things on this list as being present in her childhood and to a lesser extent in her marriage. Paul would never have physically hit her but he could be quite sarcastic and his words packed quite a punch. He refused to let her look for work off the farm for a number of years, and his parents controlled their finances. She had to ask her father-in-law for money to live on each month and even with her history of frugality and with her making most of the family's clothes there was never enough, as income was ploughed back into the farm.

A number of times Joy gave Paul a shopping list when he was going into the town fifty kilometres away; he did not necessarily buy everything on the list. He would decide that they could do without things that Joy considered essential. It was frustrating when she was expected to cook for workmen and community functions as well as the family. When Joy's family came to stay they brought their own food with them. Several times when she wanted to invite friends to their home Paul refused to have them come. On the rare occasions when they were to visit her family, the trip was almost always delayed for some reason.

Unfortunately, due to circumstances she could not control, Joy was unable to continue studying Psychology, and instead transferred to Educational Psychology. One semester she came across some research that fascinated her and she decided to follow it through for the semester. It was looking at why children who would have been expected to get into trouble with the law as they got older managed to become good citizens as adults.

A large study had followed children who had come from dysfunctional homes for a number of years. Some of these families had problems with substance abuse, psychiatric problems, violence, neglect and poverty. While not all of the children ended up in prison, many did have dysfunctional families of their own. The difference they found with those who managed to complete education, get reasonable jobs and have good families was that some-one, somewhere, had cared for them in a loving, encouraging way. It was most beneficial if the carer was in their lives for at least one year before they reached the age of ten.

The person who made the difference could have been a neighbour, a teacher or another member of their family. It could have been that the parent with psychiatric problems had a good year. Whoever it was, that person made a huge difference to the child's potential and therefore, life. It was incredible that one loving, caring person could make such an enormous difference to these children with many scars from abuses they had suffered.

Joy thought of her own life and was able to identify several people who had loved her and had treated her as though she mattered. They were her Grandma, Auntie Elsie and three of her teachers. "Thank goodness you were there for me," she thought. "Who knows where I might have ended?"

Many issues were being brought up that stirred memories from her childhood and, since she was now living in a city where facilities were available, she had counselling with a psychologist for a few months. She also went to a Sexual Assault Clinic for a while. Both of these places she found helpful in getting a better perspective on what had happened during her childhood.

Joy had to go through the usual process of selection as a candidate for ministry. Although there had hardly been a Sunday in her life when she hadn't been at church or Sunday School [She always won an attendance prize], Joy knew little of the wider church and its polities. After local and regional acceptance, those applying each year were required to attend a weekend where they were scrutinised and questioned closely.

The week before this was due, towards the end of the first year of study, Joy was told that she had a cyst on her ovary that was possibly cancerous. She knew that almost always ovarian cancer was terminal by the time it was diagnosed. She had to go for further tests after the weekend. Needless to say she was not in a good frame of mind for the selection process.

Joy found the candidating experience both bewildering and frightening. She had never before been to the retreat house where it was held, and found it difficult to find her way around the maze of rooms. Those who had partners were able to take their partners with them and all took advantage of this. There was only one other besides Joy who didn't have a partner, a woman she found somewhat overwhelming, and she and Joy were required to share a room. One woman, whose husband, a minister, had accompanied her in his dog collar, announced loudly, "This place is like a second home to me. I spent so much time as a child here with my parents." Her father was also a minister as were the fathers of several others.

Each candidate had to appear before four two-person panels and Joy found one pair particularly intimidating as they seemed to delight in confusing her with their questions. They laughed when she failed to understand what they were asking and Joy felt decidedly uncomfortable with them.

In the end, Joy was told that her candidature had been deferred due to her ill health which meant that she would need to go to the weekend again in the next year if she wanted to continue. Her own minister, who was on the Education for Ministry committee, was cross about this. "The correct thing for them to have done would have been to have accepted you subject to a clearance on your health," he said. He arranged for Joy to meet with the chairperson of the weekend to discuss what had happened so that she would feel more comfortable the next year.

There had been sixteen applicants that year, eight of whom were the children of clergy. Six of these eight were accepted and only two others. Joy wished to make a clear point that those related to clergy were at a distinct advantage as they knew many of the panel and the answers to some of the questions simply because they were ministers' children so she pointed this out to the chairperson saying sarcastically, "It seems as though they got an extra fifty points for being the children of clergy."

The irony was lost on the woman as, happy that Joy had recognised this, she answered, "Yes, yes. Here in this state we have a wonderful tradition of ministry going down several generations!" Joy found out later that she was the daughter and sister of clergy.

Two weeks later, following more tests, the doctors decided that there was no growth on her ovary, that it had been a false alarm. Twenty years later she had a benign cyst removed that may have caused the false diagnosis.

To add insult to injury, while they were at the weekend, Joy's car had been parked in an area with about twenty other cars. There had been a storm and a branch had fallen on to her car, smashing to bonnet. No other car was damaged. Joy began to have doubts about her call and this was frightening in its implications. She had given up so much to get where she was and could not go back. Thoughts of an unknown future scared her.

It took her quite some courage to face the panels again but she was accepted as a candidate for ministry the following year.

DOUBTS

"The only true wisdom is in knowing that you know nothing."
Socrates

Joy had been taught early in life was that you must not doubt God, the Bible or your faith. Doubting seemed to be an unforgivable sin in the eyes of her Sunday School teachers. The Bible said, "Do not doubt."[James 1:6-8] The moment you let a doubt enter your head, you were lost or so it had seemed that they had told her. But from the time of Paul's death, she had doubts and now she was filled with them.

To begin with she had been angry with Paul for leaving her [something she found was common to younger women who had been suddenly widowed.]. During their marriage Joy and Paul had almost never had an argument. When she had wanted to talk about something, he would walk out, saying he was too busy; that something needed attending to around the farm. This had infuriated her. His death seemed like the ultimate walk out. Joy knew that this thinking was illogical but couldn't help how it felt.

Now, when Joy wanted to argue with God, it felt as though God had walked out too. She was furious with God but couldn't turn her back completely as she believed that God had been there for her many times. Instead she began to doubt that God was like she had always pictured. She was given a book, "The Courage To Doubt". It was truly liberating as Joy read that it was okay to question, that this is how we learn. After all, children learn much through asking many questions even when they are driving adults mad. It was also about learning to trust your intuition and to have the faith in yourself to decide one way or the other or the courage to live with uncertainty.

Joy realised that she had made few major decisions for herself. She always relied on others to do this for her. Her mother had decided that Joy would study Occupational Therapy. Paul had decided that they would marry and that they would do so between tennis and football seasons so he didn't have to miss any matches. She was studying to become a minister because she believed that she had no choice other than to obey God's call. She was amazed when one of her lecturers suggested that she could have said "no". Such an idea had never occurred to her. It seemed that she had picked up little of the idea that we have the freedom to choose how we behave in all things.

Joy realised that there were a number of voices in her head that talked to her incessantly. Some told her what to do; some criticised and ridiculed her. They were not helpful and could be confusing when she was trying to decide something. One day, in an effort to examine these voices that seemed to be so much part of her, Joy wrote her full name across the top of a sheet of paper and then wrote a list of first names using the letters from her name. She was surprised how many there were. Most were female and some were male.

Joy then set about attaching a personality to each of the names according to how they spoke to her. One was the voice of Mary, her mother, another, the voice of Errol, her father. All of her sisters were represented. The neighbour who called her an inverted snob was there. Her mother-in-law was there telling her to pull up her socks, and many others, some with wise advice, others not so helpful.

Joy called them the board of directors and decided that when she needed to make a decision she would ask them for their opinions individually and then make the decision. It was a lot less chaotic in her mind than when they were all trying to get her attention at once. Joy pictured them sitting around a large table in a board room and she would go round the table listening to them each in turn. She continued the practice for several months and it was helpful for her.

Then one day, Joy noticed a child about three years old standing in the corner of the room, watching what was going on. Joy invited the child to sit on her knee and asked if she wanted to say something. The child smiled shyly but said nothing. Later Joy realised that this child represented herself.

Soon after this, Joy realised that she could make decisions with a clear head. She no longer needed the opinions of others and could work things out for herself. The board of directors were only occasionally needed and they largely disappeared from her life.

Joy talked to a psychologist about the practice and she became concerned saying that Joy had schizoid tendencies. When talking about it later, Joy said that she wasn't bothered by the psychologist's assessment, only that she, Joy, had failed to explain it in a way that the psychologist could understand. "As soon as I mentioned voices, the psychologist assumed I was psychotic. Her manner towards me changed," she said, "and the harder I tried to convince her I wasn't, the more sure she became. I wished that I hadn't told her but the process was a help to me and I thought that she might be interested."

However, when Joy spoke to her Spiritual Director about it, she said that it was a well- known spiritual exercise that had been used for many centuries to sort out how our ideas were being influenced. She showed Joy a reference to the practice in a book she had.

Even though it was hard work, Joy loved studying. There was so much to learn. She particularly responded to Liberation Theology that talked about God caring most for those that others cared least for. Perhaps her mother's constant criticism had its benefits. Joy had learned to be aware of things that were wrong or unjust and could now put that awareness to use by bringing such things to other people's notice and working to make things better for all.

Even though Joy had considerable encouragement from her minister to become a minister, the local Parish did not support her. They believed that women should not hold the position. The elders had voted for her to go forward in her candidating but after had seemed puzzled as to why they had made that decision. They gave her one donation towards buying books but then supported a male student who was studying at the same time as Joy. This fuelled her doubts as to whether she was doing the right thing.

NEXT STEPS

"Every action has its pleasure and its price." Socrates

During Joy's first year of study, the Church worked out that they had more ministers in training than they needed so they decided to implement a waiting list for placements for those studying at the moment. Because she had been deferred instead of accepted at the Candidating Weekend, Joy was to be the first person on the waiting list. This meant that she would complete her requirements for ordination in November 1996 but could not seek a placement until 1998. By this time, she would have had been studying for five years and was keen to get on with this next part of her life.

This again was a big blow for her. She could no longer work as an Occupational Therapist as she was no longer registered. She would be fifty-two by the end of the year and Marc had just started University. She would not be eligible for any sort of help from the government because of her assets but the income from them was not enough to live on. She couldn't sell them because of the way the will was set up.

All of Joy's sisters had lived overseas and Lyn suggested that she try and get work overseas if she couldn't get any in Australia. It took a while for Joy to see that this was a possibility but then she discussed it with her children and the two older ones who were by now married with children urged her to give it a go. She wrote to the Methodist and United Reform Churches in England and the Church of Scotland. The Methodist Church replied that she was of no use to them unless she could start work on September 1st which she could not as she wouldn't have finished by then. However Joy remained optimistic that someone would want her.

Towards the end of March, Joy went with Lyn while she was shopping for a new jacket. In one shop, Joy saw a beautiful, dark green, classically styled overcoat. It was magnificent; fitted her perfectly and suited her colouring. It was just what she could use if she was going to work in the UK. But her heart sank when she saw the price tag of $350. She could never afford or justify that amount. Then the United Reform Church replied that they could only offer her a part time position which would not pay for her costs. A couple of times she went back to the shop to check on the coat, just in case.

Week after week there was no reply from Scotland. Reluctantly Joy set out to come to terms with the idea that she would not be leaving Australia. It would be frivolous to buy the coat and anyway, if she was going to be unemployed she would never be able to afford it.

Then in the July, with still no reply from Scotland and her other options exhausted, Joy had a sudden irresistible urge to use all her savings and buy the coat. When she entered the small shop, she was shocked to see it had altered considerably since she had last been in it. Its shelves were lined with spring and summer clothes. The green coat was nowhere to be seen. There seemed to be nowhere that it could possibly be. There were no full length racks; only ones to fit shorter garments. Joy stood, disappointed, in the middle of the store and the woman behind the counter said, "Can I help you?"

Almost in tears at the thought that she had missed the opportunity to get it, Joy stuttered, "I was hoping that you still had a green overcoat that I had seen here. I tried it on back in March and loved it, but couldn't justify paying for it then."

The woman cut her short. "It's on the end of that rack, folded up". She pointed to where the end of the rack was jammed against the back wall.

Joy raced to the rack that had a large $50 Clearance sign on it. She grabbed the coat and was pleased to see that it had been marked down to $100. The assistant explained that someone had put it on layby and then decided that she didn't want it. "It was obviously meant for you," she said.

Joy went to hand the woman two fifty dollar notes as payment. "Oh no," she said, "It is on the fifty dollar rack. That is all you have to pay."

Joy was delighted and rationalised that the coat was compensation for the disappointment she felt at not getting work when all her friends had placements.

The weeks passed with the end of the year coming closer. In Joy's second year of study a Methodist minister from the United Kingdom had come to their college to do his PhD. He had been her tutor for Theology. In August 1996, he returned for a visit and one of the lecturers told him of Joy's plight. He found Joy in the dining room and told her that a minister from the next circuit to him, in England, had suddenly resigned leaving a vacancy that would be difficult for them to fill for two years. He suggested that Joy might like to apply for the position to help them out until that time.

By this time Joy had almost talked herself out of the idea of going overseas and the thought of going there alone to work had become scary. Unemployment scared her more. By this time, Andrew and Jess were both married and they encouraged her to "go for it" but Marc was less enthusiastic about the idea. Joy hoped that he would come and do some study at an English University, but unfortunately, that didn't work out for him.

The minister from the United Kingdom left to return home on the first Tuesday in September, taking Joy's credentials with him. At five o'clock on the following Monday morning, Joy was woken by a phone call from the Superintendent Minister of the circuit asking her if she would come there. In his enthusiasm, he had forgotten about the time difference in Australia. The people wanted her as soon as possible as their church year had started on the first of September.

This began five weeks of intense correspondence between the Uniting Church in Australia and the Methodist Church in England. The Uniting Church would not ordain Joy until she had the placement and the Methodist Church would not give her the placement until she was ordained. Finally after many phone calls, the two churches agreed to trust one another so that arrangements could go ahead.

The next few weeks were incredibly busy as Joy completed her degree and the requirements for ordination and made all the travel arrangements as well as getting a passport and working visa. She handed in her last essay on the 14th November and was ordained on the 16th.

Her father had never mentioned about burying him again so Joy had refrained from bringing it up with him. On 25th November when she was about to walk through the departure gate at the airport to fly to England to work, he suddenly said, "What about that job I gave you to do?"

"I guess you will just have to wait till I get home." She replied

Errol chuckled as she walked away and wait he did for another ten years.

Joy had an enjoyable two days in Surrey with Paul's sister and her family, before going by train to the large regional city nearest to where she was to start work on 1st December. She arrived at the Railway Station at 2:30 pm and was met by three men who were cross because she had said that the train would arrive at 2pm and they had been standing in the cold waiting for her since then. Joy had come twenty thousand kilometres and was a half an hour later than she had said. They hadn't thought to check the timetable and had only come twenty kilometres! She was a bit puzzled by their reaction.

They took her to the Superintendent's home for a quick afternoon tea where she was offered fruitcake with a slab of hard cheese, a regional delicacy. They wanted to get her to her home before dark which would be shortly after 4pm. It was freezing. There was no snow, but everything was covered with ice. The manse was not the rose-covered thatched cottage Joy had envisioned. It was a nineteen eighties purpose-built house, very plain to look at but perfectly adequate for the job. They were in the process of installing a shower as someone had warned them that Australians preferred to shower. Joy was pleased to hear this but had to be content with bathing for the eight weeks it took them to complete the work.

Her new home was in a village only a five minute walk to the North Sea Coast. It is on the same latitude north of the Equator as Cape Horn is south and she experienced some fierce gales and storms. Having never lived near the sea before, she enjoyed watching some of the wild weather from the shelter of the dunes, rugged up in her overcoat. The village had about six thousand five hundred people with twenty five per cent unemployed since the coal mines had converted to open cut mines about eight years earlier. Besides ex-miners, about half of the congregation were fisher-folk. There were some tradespeople and some who had spent their lives 'in service' in the big houses in the district.

That winter was clear and cold, blue skies and ice. In the February, someone told her, "When the North Sea starts warming up, it will be overcast for about six weeks." It turned out that it was overcast for the next eighteen months with the summer and second winter being grey, grey and more grey.

The days of December were short. It didn't get light till after nine. Joy could only get in one visit before lunch time. She quickly learnt that everyone had a cooked lunch and preparation started around eleven. She needed to leave them in peace to do this. Then they had a nap after lunch so you mustn't visit until after two. Unless they were expecting visitors, the people would not answer their doors after dark which was at four o'clock in midwinter. However, the people were always friendly, welcoming her with, "Would you like tea, coffee or a sherry?"

All Methodists Joy knew in Australia were strict teetotallers. Their forebears had come to Australia in the eighteen hundreds as teetotallers and had remained so while those who had remained in the UK had moved on from this practice. Joy had a friend who had married into a Polish family in Australia. She and her husband had travelled to Poland and on return had told Joy that the Poles in Australia were more Polish than those in Poland. She had also met a German Lutheran pastor who asked her why they Lutherans in Australia practiced nineteenth century theology. Immigrants, in an attempt to hold on to their culture, resist the natural evolution that occurs in all religions, nations and cultures.

Joy had difficulty in understanding much of what the folk said. It was even worse when she started working in the prisons. She hadn't anticipated this problem since they shared English as a common tongue. It wasn't just the accents; they used different words and phrases and had different names for things. Not long after she arrived, Joy got laryngitis and looked for cough lollies in the supermarket. It took her quite some time to establish that lollies for the English were what we called "icy poles". What we called "lollies" were sweeties and "cough lollies", lozenges. When she asked, they said that they didn't have any trouble understanding her because they watched *Neighbours* and *Home and Away* and so were familiar with her accent and the words she used [though they didn't know what a chook was]

One word that was used was 'canny'. They would say of Joy, "My, she's a canny lass!" This bothered her as she understood 'canny' to mean shrewd or crafty so she asked about it. To them it was similar to "a bonny lass". When she explained her understanding, they laughingly told her that that was how the Scots understood it.

Joy also had difficulty finding other things she wanted to buy in shops. Ingredients were packaged in smaller amounts and no one had heard of jelly crystals. Their gelatine came in blocks that looked like rubbery, coloured blocks of chocolate. To her surprise there was no pumpkin. As they had always had pumpkin with their roast meals at home, Joy had assumed that the English would eat it too but at least in the area she was, they only had pumpkins for Halloween. Swedes were the main yellow vegetable and leeks were a great favourite as well. Joy couldn't find coconut in the local shops. Then one day as part of her work, she asked a woman from London how she was settling in to this town in the North.

"Do you know, I can't find coconut anywhere here!" she exclaimed and they were able to share their frustration.

It was still in the "Mad Cow" era when Joy arrived and meat was very expensive compared with Australia and very little red meat was eaten besides pork. She was introduced to mushy peas to eat with chips and the peas-pudding of the childhood nursery rhyme. It was made of reconstituted dried peas, had a slightly green-grey colour and was solid enough to slice. It was put in ham sandwiches as we might add cheese or served as a chunk with a salad meal.

She soon developed an admiration for people who emigrated with the hope of a better life for their children, especially those who could not speak the language of their new home country. It had only taken her twenty-four hours to reach London from home and she could go home any time she wanted. She could ring her children daily. Many of those who had come to Australia after the Second World War had taken up to six weeks to get to Australia by sea and never expected to return to their home countries again. Most did not have telephones or their relatives in the UK did not so phone calls were limited to birthdays and Christmas when arrangements could be made in advance to send and receive the calls.

At a migration museum in Ireland, Joy learnt that those who had come to Australia in the eighteen hundreds had taken up to nine months to get there. Many got shipwrecked or died from illness on the way. Joy's mother, like many other Australians, had always been critical of the "whingeing Poms". Now Joy could understand why they complained in confusion, grief and homesickness as the place they to which they had gone turned out to be different from their hopes and expectations.

WOMEN'S LIBERATION

"Once made equal to man, woman becomes his superior."
Socrates

Joy was the only woman minister in the Methodist Church for all of the rural part of the county. One member of her congregation pointed out, "You are the first minister we have ever had without a beard." She found attitudes to women difficult and different from what she was used to in Australia. Some women in the county where she was still didn't have equal pay with the men. Joy commented to her brother-in-law that the English seemed to be about forty years behind Australia in women's liberation. He replied, "Have you forgotten that the state we come from was the second place in the world to give women the vote and the first to allow them to be members of parliament? The English *are* forty years behind."

In February, the superintendent minister began a study course with his congregation that was designed to read through the Bible in one year with weekly discussion groups. He told Joy that she was to attend this course. She felt a bit insulted by being expected to this forty-five week course as she had just completed five years of full time study. Later she learned that people of her age who were accepted into ministry in England only had to do two years of part time study.

At the first night of the course, there were about twenty people seated around an enormous table. The Super [that is how he referred to himself] said was, "I want you to take your Bible in your hands and ponder it for a few minutes."

Joy picked hers up and immediately a light bulb of recognition flashed through her head and she saw something she had never thought about before in spite of all her study. She had been reading this book, well not this particular copy, but others like, it for forty years and at tertiary level for five years, and this had not occurred to her in all that time.

When the Super asked them what had happened for them as they held their Bibles, he started with Joy. She has no idea what he was expecting but she said, "I realised for the first time that this is a book written *by men for men*. Not a word of it was written by a woman, and until the last three centuries, women were not permitted to read it." ("Maybe that is why I struggle with so much of it," she thought.)

"Yes, yes," he interrupted in an effort to hush her as he hurried on to the next person. It was a long time before he asked her to answer another question. But for Joy it was another one of those realisations that once you have come to it you can't easily forget and she has never since seen the Bible in quite the same way.

Joy was on a learning curve so steep that it was almost vertical. She was in a different country, working with a different denomination in a different culture from that with which she was familiar. She even thought that it might have been easier if she had become a missionary to China; at least she would be nearer home. She didn't understand some of the systems of the Methodist Church and struggled with all she was expected to do, having four congregations directly under her care as well as the prisons. Fortunately there were a number of women minsters in the United Reform Church in the area and along with several female Anglican priests they formed a 'Women in Ministry' group for which she was very grateful. They met regularly for a meal, discussion and mutual support.

PRISON

"Those who are hardest to love are those who need it most."
Socrates

Joy's placement included fifteen hours a week was as a prison chaplain, ten hours in an adult male prison and five hours in a Young Offenders' Institution that were side by side on an old Air Force base. She was assigned to work with those with life sentences and the vulnerable prisoners who included those convicted of sexual offences. There was some crossover with these as three convictions of rape and arson carried a mandatory sentence of Life. The English loved locking people up and had more lifer prisoners than the rest of Europe put together, even though their crime rate was about the same.

She had only been there a couple of weeks when she was required to attend a preliminary parole hearing for a man with three convictions for rape. There were fifteen people present at the hearing including prison, work and education officers. It was chaired by one of the prison governors. Joy was the only woman at the hearing as few women worked in the prison of more than five hundred men. The hearing proceeded with the Officer in Charge giving each one a turn to make comments as to whether they considered this man was ready for release.

All said that they were confident that if released, the man would not offend again. Joy couldn't believe what she was hearing. She had had very limited contact with this man but even in that short time she had some deep concerns. She was the last to be given an opportunity to speak. With her heart in her mouth, she voiced her concerns, explaining that the words and body-language he had used when he was with her were inappropriate and even scary.

There was a stunned silence for a few seconds and then the Education Officer said, "Oh yes, the women teachers refused to have him in their classes."

And the Parole Officer said, "Yes, we had to change from the woman officer who was caring for him."

While it was a relief when they voted not to pass him on for parole, she was angry with the naivety of the men. But the incident was also encouraging for her that those present had taken note of her comments and in doing so, may have saved women from future attack. Maybe it was just that the men didn't care or maybe they just hadn't thought about it. There were no female prison officers at that time. How could they judge how safe these men would be after release when they took so little notice of their behaviour with women?

The sex offenders were considered to be vulnerable because the other prisoners were likely to beat them up if they got a chance. They were a more diverse group than the general prisoners, with many professional men among them. They were less likely to cause trouble for the officers and so their cells were larger with better beds and they had more freedom within the prison than the general prisoners.

Joy wondered if this reflected the general opinion of the community and those in charge of prisons that sex offences were not as bad as general crimes and that sex offenders weren't really to blame for what they had done, that it was at least partly the victim's fault. She also wondered how much the sexualised, sado-masochistic humour of the British people contributed to a leniency towards perpetrators and, not for the first time, whether the male image of God and the treatment of women by the Church also contributed to these attitudes.

The statistics that she was given in England said that of every hundred reports to police of sexual attack, only three ever made it to court and only one ended in a custodial conviction. When she returned to Australia, she asked about this and was told that the numbers were 'pretty similar' here. Joy knew from her experience of working with victims that most would never consider reporting their abuse to anyone, let alone the police, and so never received justice.

When she spoke of these figures, people would say, "There are always malicious reports. Some make up a story that they were attacked to get back at a man who has rejected her." Joy knew that it takes a huge amount of courage to report such abuse, especially if it is your word against his. Experts believe that only up to five percent of reports are vexatious. So Joy would reply to such accusations, "Even if fifty percent were malicious, that leaves many victims who never receive justice."

After the parole meeting she thought that she needed to take some precautions in this atmosphere. She spoke to the prison psychologist about the work she had done with victims of sexual abuse and he then worked closely with her, always advising her to leave immediately any situation in which she felt threatened.

There was only one prisoner of whom she was truly afraid, but the authorities had good safeguards for working with such prisoners. She had a personal alarm on her belt, sat where, without moving anything but her arm more than a few centimetres, she could hit the alarm on the wall and there was always an officer just outside the door, two metres away. One of the guidelines for working with prisoners was to always sit between the prisoner and the door and to leave the door open so you could get out quickly if necessary.

Many times Joy was asked how she could work in the prisons and especially with these people. She would answer that it was part of her healing to learn to see these people as damaged individuals rather than as evil. "They are not easy to be with," she admitted. "Give me a common criminal any day!" Sometime the fact that she worked with or had worked with these people alienated her from some survivors of abuse. They could not face the idea of voluntarily being with men convicted of these crimes but thanks to that chance semester in Educational Psychology where she had learned to see how damaged some of the perpetrators were, she could do it in small doses.

There were blessings as well in the work. On Wednesday evenings, an eighty-five year old Quaker woman came to assist with the group. She was quite stooped with arthritis and walking the seven hundred metres from the gate to the chapel complex in the freezing winters was hard for her. She radiated joy and the men loved her.

One evening one of the men was mucking around. A couple of times Joy asked him to quieten down to no avail. In frustration she finally said, "If you don't behave, I won't let you come next week.' In an instant he settled down. "Oh miss," he said, "Where else can I see women?" There was nothing sexual in his remark; it was just a statement of the fact of his life.

Another time when Joy was in the meeting room alone with about fifteen men, one became agitated. Nothing Joy tried helped calm him and she was becoming quite anxious. The phone, her only means of communicating with prison officers, was in another room through two locked doors. It was a relief when two of the other prisoners said to her, "Let us take him." Joy watched as they sat with the man on the steps just outside the door. They handled him very gently and he calmed down quickly in their care. They stayed with him until the officers came at the end of the session.

Joy invited a woman with a guide-dog to come into the prison to speak with the men. One of the prisoners had been patting it and was reluctant to step aside for someone else to have a go. "I have been in for fourteen years and this is the first dog I have been able to pat in that time." The only dogs that they saw were when the drug squad did a raid and those dogs were definitely not for patting.

Joy's most traumatic time in the prisons was when two young offenders took a prison officer hostage. When she received a phone call about midnight from the senior chaplain to tell her about the siege, Joy had been asleep for a couple of hours and so was feeling refreshed. She was able to go in to relieve the other chaplain immediately. About a kilometre from the prison she encountered a police road block set up to prevent the press getting near.

The prison was locked down and in eerie darkness, except for where the incident was occurring and where the control centre had been set up. All phone lines into and out of the prison had been blocked except for one so they could be in touch with the ultimate control centre which was elsewhere in the country; maybe in London or another prison.

Joy's main task was to come to the phone at regular intervals to ring the wife of the hostage and assure her that all was progressing well towards his release. Specialist prison officers and negotiators had been brought in from other prisons in the region as well as extra officers in general in case the trouble spread to other prisoners. There was a huge black truck pulled up to the door of the wing where the control centre was, that had all sorts of technical equipment for making contact with the prisoners.

Joy was given a variety of jobs to do. Sometimes she sat in on the debriefing of the negotiators. Once she was asked to look up some details of one of the hostage takers. The first thing that caught her eye as she opened his file was that his birth date was the same as that of her son Marc, then nineteen years old. This information disturbed Joy. What was she doing in this situation on the other side of the world from her son? Had she abdicated her responsibility for him for this seeming adventure that was now more like a nightmare? If she was to believe what she had learnt, the lad who had taken the officer prisoner had had no one there for him and now Marc had no one there for him. His Dad had died when he was nine and his Mum had gone to the other side of the world on her own adventure when he was eighteen.

When she wasn't needed for a few minutes, Joy visited some of the prison wings away from the activity. She found some very anxious prison officers. There was only a small number on night shift and, because all communication had been cut, and lock-down was in force, they had no idea of what was going on. They were alone and isolated in their area of responsibility. One had himself been taken hostage ten years before and was very stressed and pleased to see Joy.

There was a squad of riot police dressed all in black waiting to storm the room if that was the decided action, and there were other police officers in plain clothes ready to arrest the prisoners when the guard was released. And a team of officers with dogs. There was only one other woman present and she was second-in-charge.

About 4am Joy sat on a narrow form and put her head in her hands. It was overwhelming. "I can't do this', she thought. "Nothing in life has prepared me for this!" And a small voice inside her said, "On the contrary, everything in your life has prepared you for this. You can do it." Reassured, she got up and got on with what needed to be done.

Joy was relieved of her responsibilities by day staff at 8am. The sun seemed unusually bright as she walked from the main prison area. In the gate building, a room had been set up for debriefing and every member of staff had to go through that room to speak with a counsellor before they could leave. Joy only spent a few minutes in there. She was too exhausted and confounded to say anything. She just wanted to get home to the security of her bed where she could pull the cover up over her head and pretend it had been a nightmare.

"The situation was resolved" as the media release put it, at about 3pm that day, with the hostage released, badly beaten but alive. As Joy walked around the prison in the days following, all she heard from the officers was anger as they felt that their security had been compromised. They no longer felt as safe as they had the previous week, before this.

A couple of days later, the senior chaplain got in touch saying that they were planning a Thanksgiving Service for the officer's safe release and would Joy like to do a prayer for the service. Joy had her doubts about how a Thanksgiving service would be accepted without some acknowledgment of the grief, loss of trust and security. Thanks to what she had learned in Pastoral Care she did a prayer of lament about having seen darkness, mentioning the sense of loss she had heard from the men and how hard it was to keep trusting in good and God in such circumstances.

Several, including one of the governors, told her afterwards that her prayer was the only meaningful thing for them in the service. This helped Joy to learn to trust her instincts about situations more.

Some months later, she was in the other prison when she saw an officer guarding a room. "Hi, how are you?" she asked breezily as she walked past.

"Alright now," he replied.

The 'now' caught her attention and she turned saying, "Now?"

"Yes," he said, "I was sent to the other prison for the hostage incident. It takes you a while to get over something like that." Joy agreed with him. It had altered her view of life as well. They chatted for a few minutes before she needed to go and he thanked her for stopping. "You can't talk to the others who haven't been through it," he said. "They just don't understand." This had been Joy's experience as well. There were ten chaplains working between the two prisons but only one other had been involved in the incident and the rest, to Joy's surprise didn't seem to understand or care.

In the prisons there were instructors who taught the prisoners woodwork, bricklaying and other trades. One of these men was having trouble with a couple of Prison Officers. It was apparent to Joy that they were bullying him. She tried to find some information on bullying in the workplace but in 1998, could only find a few books on bullying for children.

Joy's previous experience with bullying had been when she had gone to pick up Marc from his school for an exit weekend and the Master had asked to speak with her.

There had been trouble in the boarding house. Some of the boys were bullying a Chinese boy, who came to the school from his home in Hong Kong and shared a room with Marc. It must have been lonely and difficult for him being so far from home. Joy asked the master if Marc had been involved in the bullying and he had replied, "No, but neither did he stick up for the boy." Joy realised then that children not only need to see us do the right thing but also to be taught not to just stand back and watch when injustice is occurring.

About three years later, back in Australia, a school counsellor who knew of Joy's interest in this subject invited her to a seminar on bullying put on by the Education Department. Mostly it was about bullying among children but one session for the day was about adults. The presenters told of how they had attempted to start a course in a school to prevent bullying and had then realised that they needed first to address the bullying behaviour of teachers and parents before they could get anywhere with the children.

It is good that some progress has been made in naming and preventing bullying in the fifteen years since then, but as they said that day, sometimes when we address overt bullying it just becomes covert. To considerably decrease bullying in our communities would require an enormous amount of funding and energy, working with a considerable portion of the population.

There were four ministers in the circuit Joy joined, the Superintendent, who referred to himself as "the Super", a male minister from the United Reform Church, a retired minister from the Methodist Church in the USA and Joy. There were thirteen congregations in the cluster with services in the morning, afternoon and evening as well as Joy's requirement to take up to three services on a Sunday in the prisons. At least one Sunday a month, Joy had four services which she found quite tiring.

The minister from the USA had been widowed about the same time that Joy had been but Joy was constantly amazed at the way he was treated differently by the locals. The English people were very class-conscious and generally admired Americans. Joy, on the other hand, was constantly reminded that she came from the Antipodes and had come to England to learn from them. Several times the treasurer commented on how much money they were able to save because they had no obligation to pay Joy for her travel and moving costs or superannuation. The people of the church had provided a car for the American while Joy had to buy her own.

The women of his congregations could not do enough for Tom, the American. They cooked meals for him, cleaned his house and did his washing. The only help Joy got was that, occasionally, someone mowed her lawn for her.

Joy looked forward to attending a retreat for the ministers of the Methodist District in which she worked. It was to be held at an Anglican Retreat Centre in a huge old house surrounded by very beautiful bluebell woods. There were about fifty ministers present and all except Joy and a woman from a Pacific Island were given single rooms. It felt like a repeat of the weekend when she had candidated. The woman with whom she was to share the room said to Joy, "I've felt put down since I came to England because I come from an ex-colony. Now we are the only two who weren't given a room for ourselves, I know for sure that is how they see me." Joy agreed with her and was pleased she had been brave enough to mention it.

At one meal, one of the people on the same table as Joy said, "See that man over there," indicating one on distant table, "He has a degree in Theology."

"I have one, too," Joy said. Heads swung in a mixture of scepticism and awe, in her direction.

"We only get the opportunity to do a degree if we start straight from school," he said.

Once again Joy was grateful for the education that the Uniting Church had given her but it was a surprise to hear that the church leaders here had less education. In the United Kingdom, the teachers of Religion Studies in secondary schools must have degrees in Theology and Education. The subject is treated the same as other secondary subjects. Perhaps religion is taken more seriously in schools because of the link between the Church of England and the state with the Queen being the head of the church.

Joy had heard it said that Australia was a classless society. "Oh no, it is not!" she had replied. She had learnt early on when she went with her uncle to deliver fruit and vegetables to the big house in the suburb of her Grandmother's shop. One of their neighbours cleaned for these people and occasionally as a teenager, Joy had helped do the dishes after a dinner party at the homes. The size and opulence of the rooms left her speechless and the richness of their dinner crockery and cutlery amazed her.

When she had studied Occupational Therapy the matter of her "class" had come up; when she was studying Theology, one of the lecturers had commented with surprise that he had just found out one of the female students was the first in her family to tackle tertiary education - so when she graduated she would be the first in her family with a degree. Several others present, including Joy, said that this would be the same for them. The lecturer was amazed as both his father and his grandfather had tertiary qualifications.

Joy also knew from working in the Community Health service that her family were far from the poorest people, even in their two-bedroom home. But she wasn't prepared for the class distinctions in the United Kingdom. The people of her congregation spoke in awe of the various Lords for whom they worked. A nearby town of sixteen thousand people, was largely owned, as was about half of the county, a duke with the added title of Lord. A different lord owned the village including the chapel in which one of her congregations met.

Any new legislation for the country could be vetoed by the unelected House of Lords. Joy had been unaware that there were Law Lords, Judges, and Ecclesial Lords, Bishops of the Anglican Church as well as hereditary Lords and appointed Lords. One February morning, twenty seven new Lords were announced.

At a study group, the people were talking about the conditions under which they worked for a particular lord. One member of the congregation had just lost her home. She lived with her husband in a tied cottage; that is one that came with the job on the estate. Her husband had died suddenly and she had a week to find new accommodation. It was understandable for the lord's point of view that he needed the house for the new man who was to take her husband's place. But it seemed unnecessarily callous to put her out so soon. She needed to apply for Council Housing that could take months to organise.

Joy asked the group, "What do you think that it means when we say, 'Jesus is Lord' in view of how you see lords?" As she might have expected, they all said that they knew Jesus was not the same as the British lords. So she rephrased the question, "What impression does it give to those who have not had anything to do with the Church to hear that we call Jesus 'Lord'? It was something they had never thought about and was quite shocking to them. Someone commented that "Lords lord it over you. When one approaches you while you are working, you must stop what you are doing, stand to attention and remain silent unless to answer a question." Those present now thought that the term "Lord" should be used sparingly for God and for Jesus.

While in the UK Joy had heard for the first time about the Highland Clearances, where the English lords had, in effect, ethnically cleansed the highlands of Scotland in order to have more land to graze cattle and sheep and more room for hunting. She already knew that during the Potato Famine that had brought many Irish to Australia, the English lords in Ireland were exporting food produced on their land while the Irish peasants who worked the land were dying of starvation. It is possible that a number of Scottish people who came to Australia had been displaced in these Clearances.

One Sunday morning Joy was woken at 6am by the phone. It was her daughter-in-law ringing from Australia. "I thought it would be good to let you know, in case you don't have the radio on before you go out this morning that Princess Diana was killed a few hours ago." It was mid-afternoon in Australia and they had been following the story for several hours. Joy was due to take her first service at the Young Offenders' institute at 8am and probably wouldn't have heard. The boys had heard though, and were very upset.

They loved Diana. She was an idolised mother-figure to those who had not had much mothering in their lives. At a group where Joy had had a student minister with her, they were discussing the Prodigal Son and the question had come up, "What age were you when you left home?" The student had left home when she was twenty-three to marry. Joy had left home to study at seventeen and then returned for three years before she married. The last of the ten boys in the group had been away from his parents by the age of eight. Three boys had been in care from birth so it wasn't surprising that Diana had become a surrogate mother for them.

Except for prayers for the Royal Family, the services that morning were abandoned to allow the lads to talk about what the Princess meant to them. They felt strongly that she had been treated badly by Prince Charles. Joy was touched when they came up with the idea of contributing to a memorial of some sort from their meagre allowances.

Diana's death and all that happened around it led to Joy's seeing the Royal Family in a different way. She had been brought up a royalist and had strewn rose petals of the road in front of the car when the Queen had come to Australia when she was in Primary School. She had begun to be disillusioned when she realised the great divide between the rich and the poor in England and heard stories of the exploitative nature of the British Empire that they had almost worshipped in their school days.

But in the weeks following Princess Diana's death, Joy had a new empathy for the Queen. The Press was quite harsh in its criticism of her apparent neglect of a mourning country even though she pleaded that her first concern was for her grandsons who had lost their mother.

Joy saw for the first time that the Queen is really a slave to the will of the country. She was not free to be herself and grieve in the way that she felt would give her family most comfort. She had to do what "we", the general population, wanted her to do. Joy realised how selfish it was of us to want another human to be this kind of figure-head for us. And it was not only the Queen, but all her family who had to spend their lives acting out these roles for our benefit.

Joy was surprised at how militaristic the culture was in the United Kingdom. Her experience of seeing people in uniform had been limited to Anzac Day in Australia, but here in the United Kingdom, it was usual to see at least some personnel from the Army or Air-Force every time you ventured out. There was a garrison town only a few miles away and the area where she lived was flown over several times a week, at all times of the day and night, by low-flying fighter jets.

The planes usually flew over at two hundred feet but about once a week, they came down to fifty feet. Then you could see the face of the pilot. People proudly told her that they had won the Gulf War because their pilots were so skilled in low flying. The noise terrified Joy to begin with, but she noticed that even small children took no notice of the jets as they got used to them.

There was a lad in the prison, though, who hit the floor every time he heard the planes and Joy wondered what it was in his story that caused him to behave like this, especially when the others teased him for it. Because the prison had been an Air Force base it was considered an ideal target. If these planes felt so menacing when Joy knew they were unarmed, how much more terrifying must it be for those who encountered them under the conditions of war?

Many of the Prison Officers had been in the Armed Forces and so, unfortunately, had a disproportionately large number of prisoners. It seemed that they were well trained for conflict but when they were discharged, there was no similarly rigorous training for civilian life and ended up in prison for such crimes as actual bodily harm and manslaughter.

While she was working in a prison the authorities were testing all the prisoners for learning difficulties. Over ninety percent of the prisoners had some form of learning difficulty. Members of the education staff were talking about the questions asked in the tests at lunch time and when Joy said, "I could answer 'yes' to most of those questions. Perhaps this is why I have trouble reading, spelling and transposing figures." The teacher offered to test her and found that she had this disorder. Strangely it was a relief to know what the problem was. She had said of illnesses, "It is the not knowing what it is that is the hardest. Once you have a diagnosis, you know what you are dealing with even if it is going to be difficult. Now she knew that what she was dealing with was a recognisable condition she could make adaptations where necessary.

? GHOSTS

"Know yourself." Socrates

Looking back on her time in the United Kingdom, Joy says, "Going there was a crazy thing to do. It was my first placement, with little supervision, on the other side of the world in a denomination whose governance I knew little about! The people there were crazy to invite me and I was crazy to go."

She had however, learned an enormous amount. There were highs like playing in the snow with her neighbour's children, standing on the shore in a gale, listening to the lilting tones of the dialect of local miners and visiting Scotland and Ireland from where her ancestors had come. There amusing incidents such as when she went to a Chinese restaurant and ordered beef with black bean sauce. The waiter asked, "Would you like that with noodles, rice or chips?"

There were also times when she ached with the pain of loneliness, when she longed for the more enlightened attitudes to women that she was used to. She had trouble when a married man from the congregation began stalking her and then started touching her inappropriately.

Now, twenty years on, she would tell him directly to stop, but back then she was still too timid and unsure of herself to face him so instead she spoke to the Superintendent Minister. The next day the man himself rang the Super to complain about her. "She is against men," he said.

"Only ones who get too close to her," he replied. And much to her relief, the man kept his distance and never tried to touch her again.

Joy blamed herself for not being more alert to the man. Several women in the congregation had given indirect warnings about him. "Please don't have 'passing the peace' where he has a chance to hug because he fumbles you when he hugs," a small group had said. Later two women had come to her. "We never come to the Christmas morning service because he always insists on a kiss on the lips for Christmas," they said. It is surprising now to think that such a short time ago, we just put up with such behaviour and worked around it rather than confronting it.

Joy later had women in congregations back in Australia with the same request about 'Passing the Peace'. It seems it isn't only English men who abuse this ritual.

One of the highlights of her time there was being invited to speak at *World Day of Prayer* services. One was at a Catholic Church with 350 people present. Another, in a remote Anglican Church, built in the eleventh century, was the coldest service she attended. The incumbent priest believed that heating destroyed the fabric of the building so he wouldn't allow any. It was snowing the day Joy was there and fortunately she had come well rugged up. About fifty people attended, dressed as Joy was, in heavy coats, scarves, gloves and woollen caps. They had rugs around their knees. Joy felt mean when she asked them to stand and sing. Her voice came out in puffs of vapour. It seemed colder than the burial she had done in a foot of snow, but perhaps not as perilous. The snow had been trampled round the grave to slippery ice.

Joy had only been in England about three months when she was asked if she would consider staying for an extra year. It would suit the Methodist system of placements if they didn't need to replace her for another twelve months. She consulted her children who said they would agree if she would come home for her holidays in the second year which she did. She had almost thirty-three months in England but didn't see much of the country as she was working full time. Still, she saw more than some of her congregation had seen. One member had never been to the major town which was only thirty miles from the village where she lived.

Joy's home was forty miles from Holy Island, Lindisfarne, and that became a special place for her to go on retreat. It could only be reached by foot or car when the tide was low. There was a marked safe path across the sand for those who chose to walk, and a causeway had been created for vehicles with safe towers to climb if the pilgrims got caught by the tide that was said to come in faster than a galloping horse. There are areas of quicksand between the shore and the island so it is important to stick to the marked paths.

While Joy was on retreat on Holy Island, she noticed that the slates that formed the roof of the cottage outside her window were many shades of pink, purple, mauve, lilac and grey. She had only ever thought of slate roofs being monochromatic grey except for where moss and lichens had grown on them. Seeing the incredible beauty in the colour of this roof alerted Joy to notice the variations in the colour of rock around the United Kingdom. Carlisle had red rock while not many miles away in Keswick, the slate was green and the stone that parts of Aberdeen were built from was a silvery grey.

Joy joined a *Julian* group, named for Julian of Norwich, which met for meditation at an Anglican Friary just up the coast from her home. Attending their meetings and then sharing evening prayer and supper with the friars was another enriching experience. The front wall of their chapel was mainly glass and looked out across a links golf course to a bay on the North Sea. The golf course was said to be the second one created after the one at St Andrew's in Scotland which was, in fact, just up the coast a hundred miles or so. In wild weather the chapel was a spectacular place for contemplating to power of nature.

Another place that never failed to give Joy an awesome sense of Divine presence and majesty was a standing stone circle on a rounded hill top just outside the Cumbrian town of Keswick. It is now where near as big as Stonehenge but is still special. The moment Joy first walked into it she felt this. "Surely worship has taken place here for millennia," she thought. It was surrounded by higher, more rugged hills that were sometimes snow-covered. Joy returned to this place several times and was almost always alone there.

From her twenties when Joy made the decision to concentrate on life in the present rather than life in the future, she blocked out thoughts of life after death completely. Going into ministry, especially in rural/ remote England, forced her to address the issue once more. People began telling Joy stories of having seen someone they loved after the person had died. Generally it was within a few weeks of the death. Usually it only happened once. With one exception the sightings they spoke of had been a comfort and help in their grieving.

Joy heard on a science show that scientists and mathematicians now believe that there are somewhere between eleven and twenty-seven dimensions in the Cosmos. Joy now thinks that heaven may be one of these dimensions, not some distant place but coexistent here with us as God lives in our hearts.

Several times while Joy was in England, her father spent time in hospital with chest infections. Each time one of her sisters rang to tell her she would wonder if this was the time she needed to choose between Errol and finishing her commitment to the people she had come to be with. She knew that her family would expect her to fly home if he died and so each time it was a relief when she heard that he had recovered.

Then, after two and a half years, at the end of May, she had a phone call from her Mother. "Dad's dying," she said and started to sob. Joy's heart sank, not only because of Mary's words but also because of the implications for her commitment to her work. It was finishing in the August and she had been planning the way in which she wanted to say "Goodbye". When Paul died suddenly, she had not had a chance to say "Goodbye" to him and she knew that it had compounded their grief so saying goodbye had become important to her. She knew that she was unlikely ever to return to this place that had meant so much.

Joy heard one of her sisters on the phone, "Hullo, hullo," she was saying, "Are you still there?" She had picked up the receiver when Mary had dropped it. "Yes," Joy replied from her state of shock.

"Dad said something strange," she said, "You might be able to make sense of it. He said, "I have to hang on till Joy gets home." Joy had only ever told her sister Lyn about the job she had been given to do as she had been unsure of how the others would take it. At least one of them went to a church that did not approve of women ministers.

Right or wrong, now seemed the moment for disclosure. "O yes. He said I was to bury him and I told him if that was what he wanted, he would have to wait until I got home," she said.

She remembered that he had promised a party when she got home so immediately she wrote to him saying that he had better get on with the planning for it. Mary later said that he rallied from the time the letter arrived. But Joy had an anxious few months wondering if she had done the right thing, being torn between staying to say goodbye to the people that she would never see again and wanting to be home with her family.

All in all, her time in the United Kingdom was an incredible experience. The chaplains from the two prisons took her to Holy Island for a day retreat and picnic as a farewell. They gave her a small replica of the large knocker on the door of Durham Cathedral for her to put on the door of her new home. It signified to all who touched it that they had reached a place of refuge and peace.

Joy left England with an unsure future. She had written to the Uniting Church in Australia to say that she would be available for placement from September 1999 and expected that because she had given them an extra eighteen months without the pressure of finding somewhere for her, they would be happy to place her now. However, they wrote back and said that nothing could be done until she was actually back in the country.

The church in England had offered her work elsewhere, saying that they would be pleased if she stayed with them until retirement but she was feeling guilty about leaving her children and wanted to get home. She now had three grandchildren and, as Joy had commented, "It is usually the children who grow up and go overseas to work, not the mothers," she thought the time was right for her to go home even if it meant that she was unemployed.

COMING HOME

"If all our misfortunes were laid in a common heap whence everyone must take an equal portion, most people would be content to take their own and depart." Socrates

When her son, Andrew, met her at the airport one Thursday, he had a letter with a Uniting Church symbol on it. It was from the head of Chaplaincy saying that they were in desperate need of someone to do supply for three months at the major city hospital. Joy asked why he had asked her and he said, "Because you have been a Prison Chaplain." Joy lost confidence in the man at that stage. "How can he think that hospital chaplaincy is anything like prison work?" she wondered. However she started at the hospital on the following Monday morning.

About eleven on her first morning at the hospital, Joy found herself in the acute cardiac care ward. She introduced herself, and the man in the bed immediately began to cry. "Thank goodness you have come," he said. The day before, he had had a near-fatal heart attack and there was something that had happened during the war that he had never spoken of but that had worried him every day since. He wanted to get it off his chest. He had enlisted in a small country town on the same day as many other young men from the district and so they found themselves in the same company.

At some stage, they were working with munitions. There was an accident that blew the place up killing most of the soldiers. He had been one of only a handful with non-fatal injuries. The official secrets act prevented him from telling anyone what had happened. When he tried to return home, the parents of those whose sons had been killed in the incident hounded him for information he could not give and his own mother eventually had to leave the town because of the resentment that her son had survived when the others hadn't. He had lived with survivor's guilt ever since.

When she was younger, Joy had assumed that when the war was over, the suffering had ceased, but while she was in England she heard many stories of how the effects went on for many years and often for the rest of their lives. She had an uncle who had had a lung removed because of the damage done to it when he was a prisoner of war in Germany where the Germans did medical experiments on them. The man whose heart had possibly broken under the strain of his burden, started Joy thinking again about the uncounted costs of war that went on for many years and generations.

Because of memories of Paul's death, one of the most difficult times for Joy while she was at the hospital was when she was with a woman and her four primary school aged children while their father's life support system was switched off. He had been injured in a road accident. When she left the hospital later Joy had the same experience that she had had following the prison hostage incident. It was as if the light seemed abnormally bright and she couldn't quite come to terms with all the other people around just getting on with their lives. "Don't they know or care that this terribly sad thing has happened," she wondered at one level. On another level she realised that her thoughts were irrational, that they could not possibly know or care, that we can't all care about those involved in every sadness that we hear about. It would be too much to endure.

Joy was asked by a woman who was terminally ill if she would baptise her before she died. In the book of regulations, applications for baptism have to go before the elders of a congregation and there were no elders or formal congregation at the hospital. However, there was provision for emergency baptisms. The dilemma was that while there was some urgency to this request, Joy was unsure if it would be classified as an emergency. The ministers who had exited from Theological College about the same time as Joy met together every six weeks. They discussed problems they had and so Joy used this case as her problem [although she already had planned to go ahead with the baptism].

One of the ministers in the group said that she must not baptise the woman without going through the proper procedure and that closed down the discussion. Then as Joy was about to leave, the minister at whose place they were meeting came to her with a certificate of baptism and a candle, a usual gift for the one being baptised, and said, "Go to it with my blessing."

A couple of weeks later at the arranged time, the woman was brought to the Chapel by a man with a bushy beard and many tattoos, in his forties, looking like a typical bikie.

"I am her son and I want you to do me at the same time," he said to Joy.

"Well, I need to know that you have some understanding of what we are doing," Joy replied. "What do you understand of God?"

The man told her that he lived alone in an old caravan on the banks of an inland river, far from civilisation. "The one up there is my best friend," he said unashamedly pointing skywards. "I talk to him all the time. You can't live out there under the stars and with so much space and not wonder about how it all came to be."

It was one of the most encouraging baptisms Joy ever performed and his mother was delighted. There was no doubt it was very special to both of them.

During the time Joy was at the hospital, she was asked to apply for a priority placement in a parish where it had just been disclosed that a lay person of some standing in the community had been abusing women for about sixty years. The man was in his early eighties when it all came to light. She had presumed that she had been asked because of her experience with survivors of abuse.

She was appointed ahead of several other applicants and Joy felt there was some urgency to be there with the people. But then the church authorities decided to delay Joy's arrival by three months which in the end turned out to be almost five months, "So it can all be cleared up by the time that you get there," she was told.

This immediately set alarm bells ringing for her. How could *anyone* think that aftermath of *any* sexual abuse could be cleared up in *three months*, let alone one that had been occurring for so long and had so many victims?

FACING TRUTH

"To move the world, we must move ourselves" Socrates

By the time Joy arrived in the town, the person who had been handling the situation had left for an extended holiday and no one would give her any details except for the names of the three women who had initially complained, saying that it was all confidential.

Others who had come forward expected that Joy would have been given their names and told of their complaints. Soon she began to receive phone calls, to get stopped in the street and when shopping, by women saying, "Why haven't you been in contact? Why haven't you called me? I am one of the victims." And so Joy would arrange to visit them. As they told their stories, Joy became angry and frustrated with how the church had handled the situation.

The officials dissuaded the women from reporting the man to the police as the man was "elderly" and it wouldn't be fair on him. He was in his early eighties. At that time reporting child sexual abuse was not mandatory and anyway, they reasoned, the youngest one they heard of was about fifteen [near enough to sixteen] so how could you be sure after thirty years what her age had been at the time. There were no witnesses and so it would be his word against theirs.

As so often happens in situations like this, the victims were made to feel guilty that they wanted to report him. It was implied that they were unchristian to seek justice and were told that they should forgive him.

When the first accusations surfaced, the victims were ridiculed. It was said that they could not be trusted because one was the same age as the man and probably had dementia and two others were divorced and

"You can't be expected to trust the word of these women." Initially the church was more concerned for the perpetrator than they were for the victims. When outside help was offered from professional counsellors, the men in charge refused to pass the message on to the victims. The accused was a long-term friend of many of the church leaders.

Also by the time Joy got there, most of the victims had taken on board the message of not reporting the man to the police, saying things like, "It wasn't that bad. I'd feel silly making a big fuss about it." Others were increasingly cross with those in the church who they had expected would care for them but had failed to do so.

The congregation divided into those who said they believed the stories were fabricated and were angry that these allegations had been made. "He's such a nice man and he has done so much good in the district, I just can't imagine that he would ever do such things," they would cry, and those who had been groped who stood quietly with their memories, some angry, some resigned, some looking like they wished the floor would swallow them. The issue split families and friends.

One thing was obvious. The man knew how to pick the vulnerable women who would keep quiet and not fight back. While the youngest that Joy knew about had been fifteen when she had been touched, at least one indirect victim was younger. A man in his forties, the partner of another victim, wept as he told Joy how he had witnessed the man, who was related to him, fondling a young woman when he had been nine years old. The terrified look on the woman's face prompted him to try to tell his father. He received a beating and was told never to mention the incident again. His father's reaction and what he saw affected his relationship with women from then on. His life had been impacted just as much as many of the others because as a sensitive lad, he wondered if he touched a woman he would cause as much pain and terror as he had seen in the woman's face that day.

Joy was herself becoming increasingly frustrated with the church officials, mostly men, who seemed to be completely incapable of comprehending the effect of this man's behaviour on these people over so many years. It was true that she had become somewhat zealous in her attempts to try to make them see things from the victims' side. She remembered talking to the Head of Prison Chaplaincy in England about the treatment of young offenders, another subject that she felt passionate about. They had been doubling the numbers in each cell so that two lads shared a room about the size of a bathroom and they were locked into it for up to twenty three hours a day.

"Oh Joy", he had said, "Don't become cynical."

"Too late," she had cried, "I already am."

"And getting more so," she now thought.

She had heard about how after the Ash Wednesday Bushfires, extensive reviews had been held to see how Emergency Services had responded and how they might do a better job in the future. She had been part of one such review with the Red Cross in relation to catering for emergency services and survivors in remote areas after Ash Wednesday.

Joy felt that the church would benefit from such a review of this situation but was bullied and ridiculed when she tried to instigate one. She wrote a report on how she had seen the handling and submitted it to a committee who she thought would at least be interested in hearing from her perspective. Without any further communication, a member of the committee sought legal advice from the highest level of the church in Australia to see if Joy could be sued for slander for what she had written.

The answer apparently came back, "No," but Joy was not told this and was left wondering for many weeks until someone told her unofficially. She was further ostracised. Not for the first time she wondered whether how we see God has anything to do with how we treat women and victims.

Some years earlier, the Uniting Church in Australia had set up a task group to grapple with the subject of sexuality and to clarify its position on gay ministers and same-sex marriages. There had been much ill will in congregations about this. Joy couldn't understand why people felt so strongly against gays and lesbians. She had a cousin who was lesbian and Paul had one who was gay. They were both younger and so she and Paul had watched them grow up, knowing that they were different from an early age. They had just been accepted in the families for who they were.

The mother of Joy's cousin's partner lived in the town where Joy was now living and knew that Joy was friends with the couple. One Australia Day at a Community Breakfast, Joy was in a line of people moving slowly past the sausages, bacon and eggs when she heard, "Psst". She looked around and saw a tiny elderly woman next to her. "Don't look at me," she said. "Others here will not like you speaking to me. You are the new minister aren't you? I would like to talk to you." Complying with her wish not to look, Joy affirmed that she was the minister and said out of the side of her mouth, "Tell me your address and I will visit you."

It turned out that the woman had a gay son and had stopped going to church because of the horrible things that some, whom she thought were her friends, said about gay people in discussions. She felt betrayed and disillusioned because some of the most vocal had taught her son in Sunday School. Her son was a successful chef and these same people were pleased enough to eat at his restaurant when they visited the city. The woman gathered four others, most of whom had close relatives who were gay, who had also discontinued attending church because of the hurtful things that were being said, to meet with Joy.

When Joy was preparing for a church service prior to Christmas, she read the story of the angel telling Mary that she had been chosen to be the mother of the Messiah, [Luke 1:26-38], she suddenly realised that this story was a classic grooming scenario for sexual abuse.

Mary was a vulnerable girl, probably in her early teens. She was approached by a powerful male, the angel Gabriel, and told that it was special that she had been chosen for this great privilege of being impregnated by the Holy Spirit. Her vulnerability was enhanced because the Jewish people had been expecting a Messiah for about two hundred years and many young girls at the time hoped to become the mother of the long anticipated Messiah and she had actually become the 'chosen one.' These are the sort of tactics used by predators.

Joy was relieved that she had learned that it was highly unlikely that the story had happened as it is written. It is believed by scholar that the birth stories of Jesus were added to the Gospels many years later to try to explain the perceived divine nature of Jesus. But most people who heard this story did not know this or that it was the translator's bias that labelled Mary a virgin when "Unmarried woman" would have been more accurate. However, this story was trotted out each year to emphasise how women should submit to the "will of God".

From early on in the Church, Mary has been placed on the highest pedestal with girls through all generations being told that this is who they should emulate in their lives, especially her virginity. They had been told that Mary was wonderfully obedient and compliant with God's wishes for her.

An appalling thing in the writing is that it says that God set the whole thing up! Joy couldn't help wondering what influence this story still has on the way women behave and the way men treat them, around the world.

Joy was even angrier when she remembered how she had been taught, when she was studying for her degree, that the Gospel of Luke was written many years after the death of Jesus. Here, over a hundred years after these things were known, the notes that had come to help with preparation for the church service still used the traditional interpretation of this text that idolised submission and obedience in women.

The following Sunday morning, with her heart in her mouth, fearing she might be struck dead, Joy launched into the list of grooming behaviours and then pointed out the similarities with the story from Luke, asking what influence such stories might have in our culture of sexual abuse. After the two services she did that day, she had close to twenty women tell her that they had been abused. Several said how pleased they were that she had been brave enough to talk as she had.

Joy helped form a support group for survivors away from the church, with which she worked until she left the area.

Joy had been told when she applied for this placement that they were running out of money and so it was expected that she would only be there a short time. A few months into the placement she began working fifteen hours a week as an Industrial Chaplain to supplement the income. It was during this work that she came to know people of different faiths, particularly a refugee who was a *Baha'i* from Iran. She thoroughly enjoyed the discussion she had with this man as she enjoyed all of the industrial chaplaincy work.

MOVING ON

"What screws us up the most in life is the picture in our heads of what life is supposed to be" Socrates.

After three years, her time in this placement was running out as the congregations struggled to raise sufficient money for her stipend and they felt bad about this as if they were letting her down. When Joy went, they would have no minister and would have to look after themselves. It meant a time of uncertainty and a new way of being church for them.

From late in her time at College, those in authority had been saying to her, "You are lucky. You have no ties. With your children grown up and with no partner to worry about, you are free to go anywhere."

Joy had believed the ones who said that she could go anywhere back when she headed off to England, but she realised that she had been too hasty in leaving Marc and that, because she didn't have a partner, she needed to be closer to her family for mutual support. After being on the other side of the world, her first placement in Australia was four hundred and fifty kilometres from both her sons and her daughter who were, in turn, six hundred and fifty kilometres apart. She had spent several fortnights of leave time travelling first to one lot and then to the other with all the catching up necessary; she would arrive back from leave exhausted. She wrote to the Synod asking to be placed nearer to the city where her sons lived.

The time preparing for the end of her placement was again stressful, in part because of leaving people she had worked so closely with and partly because of the uncertainty of her future. As the Synod supplied cars for those in placement, Joy had not owned a car since she had been back in Australia and so now needed to get one. Her son-in-law, David, who worked as a mechanic at a dealership, was tasked with the job to find a suitable one. It was expected that this might take a while. In the church service one Sunday, Joy had jokingly said that she hoped to get a car that matched the colour of her trusty, much admired, dark green overcoat.

On the Tuesday, she received an excited phone call from David: "Nan," I think I have a car for you. It has just been traded in. It has its full service history with us…" On and on he went telling her all about the car. When Joy could finally get a word in, she asked, "What colour is it?" "Dark green," he answered, "about the colour of that coat of yours."

Through tears of amazement Joy said, "It's my car. I will take it." Joy saw this coincidence as a sign that all would be well and she knew that it would also be seen by the people who were feeling that they had let her down, as a sign that she was being looked after and would be okay. As fewer people have been attending church and congregations have become older, Joy has known many congregations to have suffered with feelings of guilt, shame, disappointment and failure as they have no longer been able to support a minister.

MORE NEW HORIZONS

"The really important thing is not to live, but to live well. And to live well means, along with more enjoyable things in life, to live according to your principles." Socrates.

The first communication back from Synod about future work was a phone call asking her to consider going to Kununurra in the north of Western Australia. It seemed to prove to her that they had taken no notice of her plea to be nearer her family and the city. She went to Kununurra for three months' supply and again it gave some completely new experiences as she also had a stopover in Darwin for a few days on her way home.

About one third of the population of the town comprised indigenous people and Joy had had very little contact with indigenous people. As she was walking at the edge of the town early one morning she could hear them calling through the bush. Joy had an overwhelming feeling that this was their country and that she and all other Anglos had no right being there. "Not only did we steal their children, we stole their country and their dignity as well," she thought. Joy bought several books from the local store about indigenous issues and telling Dream Time stories so she could learn more about their culture. The local congregation had almost nothing to do with these people. Frontier Services provided Aged Care for some. At the request of the staff of the Day Care Centre, Joy invited some to her home for morning tea.

Ten people came, all indigenous, with one 'Anglo' carer. Most spoke heavily accented English. One elderly woman paused at the door, surveying the room. Then she almost galloped across the room to the chair next to a table on which the books were stacked. She managed to fling aside her walking frame, grab a book and sit in one motion.

Joy was fascinated by her apparent hunger for books. She ashamedly admitted that she had assumed that these people would be illiterate. The woman barely paused long enough in her devouring of the books to drink her tea. At one stage she called Joy over and pointed to where the book had a story about the last massacre of indigenous people that had occurred in the Kimberleys. She managed to make Joy understand that some of them had been her relations and Joy was further ashamed when the woman showed her a photo of indigenous men in shackles.

When a second visit was arranged, Joy bought a couple more books. One was aimed at primary school aged children. It was a beautifully illustrated story of the life of an indigenous woman. Joy justified her extravagance at buying the books by saying that she could use them later for presents. As she had anticipated, when the old woman arrived for morning tea, she went straight to the books again.

Joy's parents-in-law had taken a three-year-old of mixed Anglo-Indigenous race, Flora, to live with them in the 1960s. She was still part of the family and loved drawing. Joy thought that she would give the illustrated book to Flora and suggest that she might like to attempt something similar. Several weeks after returning home, Joy dropped the book off at Flora's. She was not at home but soon after Joy got an excited phone call from her. "That book you left here was illustrated by one of my sisters who lives in Central Australia," she said.

During the next two-and-a-half years, Joy did other supply work that lasted from four weeks to one year, in seven different places, in city and country. Back when she had first been in England someone from Australia had asked her if the people were different from here. "Yes and no", she had replied. "Each person is unique but the same things please them and hurt them wherever they are." That day a man in his sixties had told her how his father had died when he was seven and how excluded he had felt. He could not recall having been told about the death, just that he had been sent to a neighbour's house. He had sneaked into the front room of the neighbour caring for him and watched as his father's body had been taken from his home for the funeral.

A woman in her nineties had told how her only daughter had died at nine months of age. Both things were still painful for them all these years later. There is a saying about each person's pain being unique and from Joy's experience she would agree with this. It is the causes of pain that are similar almost everywhere she has been.

Three times Joy has taken part in the funerals of young men, aged from fifteen to twenty-three, who have killed themselves. The grief of the mothers has been almost inconsolable. She has seen the agony of a father as he and his wife struggled to come to terms with their much loved daughter transitioning to become their son. So much of the pain comes from wondering what others will say. And she has been with an older couple when they were advised to abort their first child. "That wasn't a decision we ever had to make since there was not the technology to find developmental abnormalities when we were younger," she comments.

Once when Joy was visiting her daughter, Jess, her son-in-law David, was being rude to her. She said, "If you don't treat me with respect, I shall come to live here and haunt you forever." Jess and David looked at each other.

"What is going on?" Joy asked.

"Well, we have actually been wondering if you would like to build a granny flat here," they said.

They had just built themselves a home on nearly a hectare of land, so there was plenty of room. David showed her a plan of the garden he had made with a path labelled, "Out to Pasture Lane" that would lead to were her place could be put.

In two thousand and four, they built a cottage in their back yard for Joy. It would make her stays at their home easier. Before this, when she visited, one of the children would have to vacate their bedroom for her and she never felt comfortable staying more than a few days. It was good to have the freedom that this separate dwelling provided.

In winter, when Joy was staying with Errol and Mary the concerns she had had for Errol's welfare sharply increased. He had had several small strokes and had some resulting dementia. He was okay with most conversations but seemed less able to care for himself. Mary had commented that she was not giving him some of his medication as she had decided "it wasn't doing anything for him". One cold evening when the three of them were sitting in the family room, Errol had said a couple of times that he was feeling tired. When he said it again, Joy said, "Would you like to go to bed?"

"Yes," he replied.

She turned to Mary, and, thinking that Mary helped him with this, said quietly, "Could it be that he can't remember how to get to the bedroom?"

Mary snorted but took Errol and then returned to the room about ten minutes later. Joy assumed that Mary had put him to bed and so was surprised, when she was going to bed later, to see Errol sitting dazed and naked on his bed with his pyjamas in a heap on the floor.

Joy said to Mary, "I thought you had put him to bed."

"No", she said sharply, "I like to give him a chance to do it for himself." From what Joy had just seen, she would have assessed Errol of being incapable of that level of self-care. Maybe that evening he was having another slight stroke.

Having worked in the field of Aged Care, Joy knew that Mary's actions in withholding medication and the neglect shown this evening could both be called Elder Abuse. Errol had a doctor's appointment for later in the week and so Joy rang the doctor. She explained who she was and voiced her concerns, adding. "I know my mother is a highly intelligent woman. At eighty four she is still capable physically and mentally of caring for Dad, but she is no nurse, isn't coping emotionally and seems to resent his dependency."

To her surprise, the doctor tore strips off Joy. "How dare you ring me and make these accusations. It was none of your business," he said.

Joy headed home the next day, determined to discuss Errol's care with her sisters but she didn't need to. Two days later Mary rang after they had been to see the doctor. "Dad's been put in hospital for assessment for care", she told Joy. He went from hospital to an Aged Care Facility. Almost immediately they heard that he had had to be reprimanded several times for groping female carers and being impossible with the male ones they gave him to protect the women. As is often the case, the women residents thought that he was wonderful and wouldn't have a word said against him.

That year was Joy's sixtieth. She finally sold what remained of their farm. She, Andrew and Jess had been ready to sell it for some time but Marcus didn't seem to be able to let go. Eventually Joy realised that his reluctance was to do with the fact that this area of land was where Paul had been alive. She talked with Marc about this and they arranged for the whole family to spend a weekend there. They went over most of the property, saying good bye and remembering the great times, lighting fires and cooking damper. It was nearly as hard as to leave this place as it had been to say goodbye to Paul only that time it had come suddenly and they had no choice.

The pain of losing the farm was tempered a little when they got a better-than-expected price for it and after paying off the not inconsiderable debts, Joy was able to think about buying a house in the city to be her retirement home. She had lived in over forty houses since Paul's death, some rented or provided by the church, and was excited to have this new home. Her children were also pleased that at last there would be a house they could relate to as a family home. Soon after Paul's death, a neighbour had said, "You don't need a house any more. With your older two about to leave home, all you and Marcus need is a unit it the city." As soon as the man left, a very serious looking Marc said, "Mum, please don't ever get a house without a lawn." Joy took this to be his nine-year-old way of saying, "I want room to play outside."

Now Joy realised that for fifteen years, she had been moving and Marc had really not had anywhere to call home. So it wasn't surprising when, not long after the sale of the farm her children set out to get a family home. Joy was working a couple of hundred kilometres from the city. Jess and David had come from their home interstate for a weekend with Andrew and his family and Marcus. To her amusement, they told Joy that they were going house-hunting for her on the Saturday.

About mid-afternoon she got an excited phone call, saying that they had found one they all agreed on. It was in the right area, not far from Andrew's home. It had a large undercover patio area and they suggested that the first thing Joy bought was a table large enough for at least a dozen people to sit around so they could all be there together. Joy had not realised how much they had missed having a family home. It reminded her of what her choice to be a minister had cost them.

Mary's home was in need of extensive repair so, after talking it over with her sisters, Joy suggested that Mary share her new home. It would also help Errol feel more settled in the Aged Care Facility as he worried about no longer being there for Mary. Mary embraced the idea with vigour. A couple of times she had said that what Joy needed was a wife to look after the home while she ministered and now Mary saw herself as filling that role. Joy had previously discouraged these ideas as unworkable and probably should have trusted her instinct this time.

HOUSE SHARING

"Everything is plainer when spoken than unspoken." Socrates

One of the problems after you start addressing issues such as the ones in Joy's life, is that from then on questions and doubts continue to pop up to be considered and, hopefully, dealt with. After Joy had left home at seventeen, her mother became a Guide Leader and, on a number of occasions, her father went with her to camps. Joy does not know if he touched any of the girls. He could be quite charming and was popular with other leaders. People commented that he had "a way with women".

In her early sixties, one of Joy's sisters went to the fiftieth wedding anniversary celebrations of Fred and Margaret Walters who had been friends of her parents for many years. The children of each family had been friends since their teen years. Sometime during the afternoon, Sandra Walters was talking to Joy's sister, Dianne.

"Look at your father flirting with Kate, [her fifteen year old daughter] just like he flirted with us when we were teenagers."

Dianne laughed as she told Joy, but it made Joy feel sick. For so long she had been telling herself that she was the only one he had touched and trying to block any other possibilities from her mind. She had watched Errol closely with her own children but he seemed disinterested except to criticise them.

Not long after, Joy and Annie were alone together at the new house, unpacking their mother's crockery when Joy suddenly surprised herself by saying, "I think that Dad sexually abused me."

Annie's sharp reply came back immediately. "Well, of course he did!"

Joy was at first puzzled by this reply. It was not at all what she had anticipated in the years she had rehearsed saying something to one of her sisters. Joy just stared at Annie who went on, "You must remember how he had erections when we were in bed with him, and mum saying in a whiney voice, "Errol, don't do that.""

This totally shocked Joy. She *hadn't* consciously remembered that part of it but in an instant, the memory was there. It must have been hovering in her sub-conscious. She remembered also how her father strutted naked around the house and how, when she was about eight this had suddenly stopped.

Mary had said at the time, "Annie [who was probably close to ten at the time] told me that she was embarrassed to see her father naked."

A relieved Joy had thought, "Thank goodness for Annie."

Now Annie's comment made sense of Joy's behaviour and apprehension about her children getting into bed with her husband or any other adult and her unease when adults sexualised children's nakedness.

For a few seconds they just stood there looking at each other before Joy said softly, "For twenty years I have been convincing myself that I would have been the only one." Now there was a sense of relief that she hadn't dreamt it all but also a flood of guilt. What might her father have done in those twenty years that might have been prevented if she had spoken out earlier?

They talked about having kept the secret and how Annie still did not want her husband or children to know.

"What about the others?" they both asked at the same time, thinking of the rest of their sisters. Together they worked out a plan whereby Joy would gather some information about where they might get help as she knew of centres in cities and regional areas where appropriate help was available and books that they may be interested to read. Then Annie would speak to Dianne and Joy would speak to Lyn. After that, the four of them would meet to talk about how they would speak to Maureen, their middle sister who they thought might have had the worst time of the sexual abuse. She had been their father's favourite but had alienated herself somewhat from the others in recent times.

They feared most for Maureen's daughter, Mandy. Maureen's marriage had broken down about the time her daughter had been born and they had lived with her parents for a number of years from when Mandy was twelve months old. Errol and Mary had looked after Mandy while Maureen studied for a degree and she had told the children at kindergarten that he was her dad.

Neither Dianne nor Lyn had any memory of sexual abuse although when Joy said about their mother's comment about their father being a passionate man and that Mary in saying it, might have been giving her an opportunity to talk about her abuse, Lyn said, "She said that to me!" She had been puzzled by the comment and Joy's theory made sense in this context even though she couldn't remember anything happening.

Maureen refused to take part in any conversations about it or anything else to do with her childhood. She lived a reclusive life for several years before attempting to kill herself. She remains very secretive about personal things but has now had several years of intensive psychotherapy and is managing life better.

However, the talk about their childhood gave the younger ones an opportunity to tell Joy that they had lived in constant fear that their parents would kill her with their beatings. They spoke of cowering in the corner to avoid the backlash of the cane and strap and of not daring to do anything because they were afraid of the same thing happening to them.

Joy was surprised by this. She hadn't thought about her behaviour impacting on the young ones like this. In some ways what they said vindicated her thoughts that she had had a rough time of it. But it also added to her guilt and shame. If she had been able to behave better they would have had a happier childhood.

Lyn talked about how, after Joy left home to study, she became the 'whipping boy' which was something else Joy had not realised. The sisters that would talk about it said they felt sure their children had not been touched, but they weren't willing to ask them and also asked that it be kept a secret from their husbands and children because two were scared that their husbands might attack their father if they knew and the other was unsure of how her husband would react. Joy felt that her children had a right to know and she wanted them to be free to tell her if they had been abused so they could receive help needed. They said that there had been nothing sexual but spoke of how awkward they felt when Errol sneered at the boys and how Mary was intolerant of them all.

About five years later, Lyn's husband left her and after another couple of years, she said to Joy one day, "I'm beginning to have memories, but I don't want to talk about it at the moment."

Mary shifted into Joy's new house in October and when Joy had finished her supply in a country town at the end of December, she too shifted into the house as she then had twelve months' supply work in the city.

Six months later, in June 2005, Errol died and Joy got to do the job she had been given by him to do. It came at quite an emotional cost that her sister's didn't and couldn't understand. From the time he had said, "You can bury me", an order, not a request, she had struggled with being distant from where he lived. She had spent most of the time since that day, hundreds of kilometres from her parents but this year, she was in there. Errol had been in an Aged Care Facility for several years and Mary was living in Joy's home.

Mary regularly attended church and the minister came to visit following Errol's death.

"I don't know why she has come," Mary snapped at Joy. "She knows you are here."

"Mum," Joy said, "I am your *daughter*, I cannot also be your minister." But Mary wasn't listening.

About a fortnight later she told Joy, "I went to arrange for a prepaid funeral for myself today. When they asked if I wanted to pay for a minister, I said 'No, thank you. I have one in the family.'"

Joy was cross with the assumption and thought, "She has her own minister at the church she attends. I hope she doesn't die for a while. I could not do it at the moment."

CONFIRMATION

"Understanding the question is half the answer." Socrates

Joy had always felt that she wasn't wanted by her parents. Her father, Errol, had been interstate in the Air Force when she was born. When she was three months old, he had passed through her home town on his way to be shipped overseas. He had three hours with his wife and daughters that day and Joy thinks that she was probably not top priority. He returned home when she was two and a half years old. Her mother, Mary, was always there for her physically but not emotionally. Joy cannot remember ever being held or hugged by her mother until she, Joy, began hugging people after her husband, Paul, died and the whole family responded.

In her mid- sixties Joy had plucked up courage to ask Auntie Ellen, her father's sister, about feeling that she wasn't wanted. Ellen had boarded with Joy's mother Mary's family for some time during the War. Joy had a good relationship with her and she felt sure that she would have known about the circumstances around her birth. She also trusted her to answer truthfully. Joy had thought about asking Mary's younger sister, Auntie Edna, but could not trust her to be honest about such a thing. She liked things nice and probably would have denied it outright even if she did know it was true.

It may seem that for Joy to have asked her mother would have been the obvious solution but there was no way Joy could bring herself to ask her. She couldn't trust herself to have such a conversation with her mother without getting angry and frustrated. If Mary denied what Joy felt, as she was likely to because she had a history of denying things she didn't want to deal with, Joy would probably raise her voice and that would get her nowhere.

Joy regularly visited Auntie Ellen but still it took her several months to pluck up the courage to ask her. One day after some casual chatter, she braced herself and said as calmly as she could, "I have always felt that I wasn't wanted from the time I was conceived. Can you tell me if this was true? It's hard to continue to live with these feelings."

A shocked look crossed Auntie Ellen's face before it softened into a sad smile. There was a moment's silence as she just looked at Joy, searching her face. Then she reached out and resting her hand on Joy's arm said, "Oh Joy, many children weren't wanted during the war. The future was so uncertain but most were loved after the War, when things had settled down." Joy didn't probe. Her aunt had said enough. She had caused her pain in even raising the question and she was satisfied by the way Auntie Ellen had said "most", that her feelings were justified.

She remembered that many years before, when she had been in her early teens, and she had been in trouble yet again, she had shouted at her father as he had come at her with the bamboo cane, "Don't blame me for the way I am! I didn't ask to be born!" The comment had momentarily stopped him in his tracks before he laid into her yet again. She seemed to have hit a raw nerve in him and she now wondered if her mother had also given him a hard time for producing this troublesome child.

Mary had come out with one of her unexpected statements about a year or so earlier, suddenly announcing, "It was your father's idea to call you 'Joy'." Joy was surprised by this and didn't know how to answer so she said nothing even though she was wondering what was behind the comment. It didn't seem to be relevant to the conversation they had been having at the time. Joy hadn't complained in recent years though she hadn't particularly liked the name as a teenager. It seemed by her tone of voice that Mary was saying, "Don't blame me for it; I had nothing to do with it."

It was interesting, though, that he father, Errol, had chosen the name as he had never called Joy by it. As far as she could remember all he ever called her was "Fat" or "Number Two." Only her third sister, number four, escaped these demeaning labels and, when the other girls discussed this, they thought it was likely to have been because she was a sickly baby and young child. Whoever it was that had first said, "Sticks and stones will break my bones but names can never hurt me!" really had no idea of the power of names. Joy could tolerate being called Number Two, but the one that really irritated was when he called her, "Matie, my little mate!" Under her breath she would scream. "I am not your mate! I am your daughter and that is not the same!"

Several months after she had spoken to Auntie Ellen, Joy was again staying with her parents when Mary suddenly said, "It was your father's idea to have you. He had notification that he was to be shipped overseas with the Air Force and thought it would be a good idea for me to have another child, to be a companion for Annie if anything happened to him." Joy suspected that Auntie Ellen had told Mary of her questions.

Joy thought about this. Annie, her older sister, would have been less than six months old at that time and Joy could imagine that her mother may not have been pleased by this suggestion. She thought that probably the last thing that Mary wanted to be saddled with, if she were widowed, was a second child to look after.

Joy could understand this because when her third child, Marcus, was born some years after her first two, a number of people had commented that she should have another child to keep him company. She was barely coping with life at the time and thought, "No thank you!" each time it was said. When Paul had died suddenly Marcus was nine years old and Joy had so much on her plate after this that she was very grateful she didn't have an even younger child also to look after.

Joy was relieved to hear the explanation from her mother. It absolutely validated the feelings that she had lived with all her life. She had seen enough wild-life programmes to know how the main aim of the male of the species is to reproduce as many times as possible before he dies. Men going to war and therefore facing the immanent prospect of death would have been no different from these animals and this is why she had come into being. Her mother's words made sense of her thoughts and feelings.

MOVING AGAIN

"To find yourself, think for yourself" Socrates

As the year went on it became more apparent that Joy and Mary would struggle to live in the same house long-term. Mary had had her own kitchen for 63 years and Joy for thirty eight. They weren't good at sharing. During winter, Mary liked the heating on 23 degrees; Joy, who had lived most of her adult life in cooler places, preferred eighteen degrees. She wished that she hadn't suggested that Mary move in and thought that it had been a mistake to shift her in before she herself had moved in. Mary seemed to love the place. She had an en-suite bathroom, plenty of room for her craft and was still driving so was quite independent.

It had become increasingly unlikely that Joy would get a placement within commuting distance when there were so many younger and more experienced ministers who wanted to stay in the city. In the July school holidays, she was visiting her daughter, Jess, who lived in a large rural city interstate. Joy was somewhat frustrated about her uncertain future. It occurred to her that if she couldn't get a placement close to her boys, perhaps she would find somewhere near her daughter. It was on her mind when she went to a large shopping centre in the city while Jess was at work. She saw a man who looked like a minister and on speaking to him found out that he was indeed a Uniting Church Minister and that she was likely to be well received in that district if she wanted to work in that area.

When Joy broached the subject of shifting interstate with her sisters, they all said that they could not have Mary living with them without resorting to violence. They were pleased that they no longer needed to worry about the repairs of Mary's home. They encouraged Joy to shift and to leave Mary in her house. "You have provided her with a new house where she is happy. You have done your bit. We will be here for her," they said.

Joy shifted to live in the cottage next to her daughter and son-in-law early in the 2006 and began doing supply, which is short-term part-time work, immediately. Fifteen months and three lots of supply later, she got a placement sixty kilometres from her daughter's home. She retired from this placement four years later when she was almost sixty-seven and immediately began doing supply work again. Most of her friends and family had done trips around Australia or gone for cruises somewhere in the world when they had retired. But Joy had learned when she lived in England that there is not much fun in being a tourist alone. She didn't fancy going with a group and so decided that she would see some different places by doing supply work. This she has done almost continuously in the last five years.

Maureen is a teacher in a large country town and she stayed with Mary through every school holidays and about one weekend a month. Lyn lives in the same country town and comes to the city frequently on business and she also stays with Mary. Joy came approximately every eight weeks to catch up with her sons and stayed at the house.

HERITAGE

"I pray thee, O God, that I may be beautiful within," Socrates

Joy has been puzzled by her heritage. There have been times when she has felt scared by it. She has heard comments many times, "Like father, like son." Or was it in her case, "Like father *and* like mother, like daughter?" She was quite flirtatious as a teenager and swung between this behaviour and rigid morality. She has never, ever sexually abused anyone, [except if you could call her non-disclosure to her husband of the abuse, abuse]. She had made sure of that. And she had not called her children by derogatory names. But to her endless shame, she did yell, criticise and beat them, especially Andrew, though not as severely, as she had been beaten. She had never learned any other way of discipline and it took her years to realise that there were alternate ways of raising children to be good citizens.

Errol told his daughters on many occasions, "If you can't find something nice to say about people it is better not to say anything at all." He said it at appropriate times when they were criticising or otherwise putting someone else down but Joy came to realise after a while that this comment was as much directed at Mary as it was to his daughters. Her mother constantly complained about people, especially Errol, and pointed out their shortcomings. This was something Joy learned well as she, too, had become more and more judgemental as an adult.

It seemed that if Mary suspected that Joy liked someone then they would receive extra attention in this way. One who was singled out was Auntie Edna, her mother's younger sister, for whom her criticism was endless. This was tiring and confusing for Joy as she liked Auntie Edna and it didn't help her to love her mother any more. This behaviour still continues with her criticism of Joy's sons even though they do more for her than any of her other grandchildren. This has eased somewhat as she has transferred her criticisms to their partners and her great-grandchildren.

When Joy's oldest granddaughter was about ten, she had been doing a cross stitch Christmas decoration. It was a lot of work and Joy was impressed at how well she was doing the work and how she was getting on with it. Joy still had several unfinished cross work items from her younger days. She said to Molly, "Show your work to Grandma," thinking that as a former dressmaking teacher, Mary would also be impressed. A moment later she was horrified as she watched her mother pick up a pair of small scissors from the table and begin to cut into the work.

"You did the crosses the wrong way in this row," she said as she snipped. "They have to come out!" she said oblivious to the distraught look on Molly's face.

Shocked at the violence of her mother's actions, Joy screamed, "Mum, she's only *ten*," as she gathered the weeping child into her arms.

"Yes, and she needs to get it right! The sooner she learns the better!" Mary snapped back.

Unfortunately no amount of persuasion could get Molly to touch that or any other cross stitch again even though Joy tried for several years.

A couple of years later Joy had forgotten about the earlier incident. She was teaching her nine-year-old grandson Luke, to use a sewing machine and he was making a cushion in a log cabin pattern in his football club colours. Again Joy was pleased with his progress and suggested that he show it to Grandma who was in the next room. He grabbed it and ran to her saying, "Look what I've done, Grandma!"

Joy entered the room in time to see him wilt as her mother said with a glare, "This row is crooked," as she stabbed her finger at the offending row with a look of disdain. She handed it back to him without another word.

"Only a little bit. It's not bad for a beginner," Joy muttered to Luke as she ushered him out of the room as she remembered the soul destroying effects of criticism.

"It's alright, Nan," Luke said quietly to Joy, "It's just Grandma. That's what she is like."

Joy first came across the "Strengths Approach" when she was learning to counsel couples for marriage. The couples were asked to complete multi-choice questions designed to identify their abilities and gifts and then to strengthen these parts of their lives in their marriage. This approach was a shock to her as her life had been concentrated on identifying weaknesses in herself and others and trying to eliminate them [without much success most of the time]. Consequently she only half-heartedly embraced this idea.

Fifteen years later, she had a supervisor from an organisation where the whole workforce ran on this approach. The supervisor encouraged her to own her own strengths which wasn't easy given her upbringing, and then to start identifying and encouraging others in theirs. It was a significant changing point for her as she looked also at how the idea that we are all sinners had impacted on her self- image and her critical nature.

Joy became convinced that when people were given freewill, God had made a pact that they would be "fore-given"; what we now call forgiveness. Using the story of the "Return of the Prodigal Son" [Luke 15:20b-24], she is sure that God does not wait until people ask for forgiveness before granting it. Joy is sure that the forgiveness is already there for us to accept and get on with life. God doesn't dwell on what we have done wrong. It is the Church that uses people's ability to make wrong choices to control people through fear and shame.

REFLECTING

"Wonder is the beginning of wisdom." Socrates

When Joy had been at Theological College, one lecturer had told them several times: "Contrary to popular opinion, we do not learn from experience. If we did, we would not keep making the same mistakes. We only learn by *reflecting* on our experiences."

Though she had become quite good at reflecting, every now and then Joy needed to remind herself again to do it. As she thought about why she had suggested that her grandchildren show Mary their work, she realised that all her life she had been trying to win her mother's approval and it seldom worked for long. Twice she had succeeded. Once when she became an Occupational Therapist and then when she was ordained as a minister. Those things had pleased her mum but she couldn't think of anything else she had done that had brought joy to this unhappy woman.

She realised that Mary had been unhappy for all of Joy's life. Her husband, Errol, was an obvious disappointment to her most of the time although their relationship did get on a bit better after they had both retired. Had they married too hastily? Was the difference in their education levels more of a problem than had been apparent? Several times Joy had heard her mother state that she came from a family of small business owners. She had not said it, but the implication was because her husband was a tradesman, it was a mistake to think that she came from the same stock.

Mary was highly intelligent especially in the area of mathematics and Joy often wondered what she could have become if she had had the opportunity for a tertiary education in the maths and sciences instead of dressmaking. Unlike most women of her time, Mary owned the house in which they lived. She had had it built just after the war finished and before Errol came home from Japan.

It was not that Errol was stupid. His motto was, "You can learn something new every day." He was interested in nature, was a member of the Field Naturalists' Society and had a particular interest in native plants. He had a large orchard and vegetable garden and a great believer in compost and earthworms before they became fashionable. At eighty-four he meant to enrol in a gemstone class but when he arrived at the venue he found he had mistakenly enrolled in an oil painting class. Undaunted, he exclaimed, "Well, I always meant to give painting a try!" He did quite well that year and would have continued the next had not a stroke stopped him.

There was a lack of generosity in her mother's spirit. She seemed incapable of giving praise, giving people the benefit of the doubt or of welcoming people into her home. Errol was a skilled fisherman and caught and froze a plentiful supply. He also loved providing a fish meal for his children and their families. Mary couldn't stand the smell of uncooked fish so she would come into the kitchen after he had cleaned up from cooking the fish to cook the chips.

Once Errol was preparing such a meal for all his children and their families and there were nine teenage grandchildren present. Mary took a large packet of chips from the freezer and counted out the chips for them and then put the packet back in the freezer. When she served up, she gave the adults about six chips each and four chips for each child. This behaviour was quite bizarre. When Lyn commented to her mother that her daughters could eat more, Mary said they would have to make do as there were no more cooked. Lyn attempted to take the chips from her plate and give them to her daughters. Mary refused, snapping angrily that Lyn had taught them to be greedy. Lyn hastily warned her sisters not to say anything but didn't have time to alert the young ones.

It would have made quite an entertainment had they been able to capture on film the antics of the parents as they tried to hush the protesting teenagers with glares, whispers and kicks under the large table. It would have been comical if it hadn't also seemed such a tragic statement about their mother. They all left her home as soon as possible after the meal and headed to the nearest fast food outlet to feed their hungry offspring.

There seemed to be no explanation of why Mary behaved like this. It didn't help the family to like her. When Joy had been studying Occupational Therapy, someone had told her, "There are generally three reasons why we don't like people. One is that they know something about us that we wish they did not, something that shames us. The second is that they reflect something in ourselves that we do not like. And the third is that we simply don't know the person so if you don't like someone, first try getting to know them better. You may not like them more but you will come to understand why you are unable to like them." This, Joy found, could be easier said than done if the person is secretive about those aspects of life which impact most on their personalities and behaviour as Mary tended to be, when asked.

What Joy did know about Mary was that the brother immediately older than her gave her a hard time and the family suspect that if he was young today, he would be found to be somewhere on the Autism Spectrum. Mary's mother had always busy trying to make a living for the family. Mary was also jealous and critical of her sister who was the youngest in the family and had been spoilt by her mother and older brothers. She had also 'made a better marriage' than Mary and so had more money for holidays and other possessions.

Recently, when Joy had been talking to someone about child abuse, the other woman had said, "That's been taken care of since we've had mandatory reporting. If a child is taken for medical attention with suspicious injuries these days, it would be immediately referred to Child Protection. And teachers are obliged to report behaviour they think indicates abuse. But Joy had never received medical attention for the abuse that she endured as she was at school before behaviour was seen in this way. This didn't mean that she wasn't scarred by it. In her mid-sixties she was sent to a specialist audiologist for investigations because she had tinnitus, ringing in her ears, and problems with her balance. Not long after he began examining her, the doctor asked, "Have you ever had a head injury?"

"No", she had replied.

A few minutes later he repeated his question and she repeated her answer. As if he hadn't heard, a few minutes later again, he stopped what he was doing, looked her in the eye and said,

"Are you sure you have never had brain injury?"

"Well," she said with a flash of insight, "My father frequently gave me back-handers that nearly knocked me over and he often threatened to knock my block off. I wouldn't have been surprised if he had!"

"That would have done it!" the doctor exclaimed.

These back-handers are also probably responsible for the arthritis in her jaw and at the base of the skull and even for the damage to her thyroid gland for which there had been no explanation.

Joy realised recently that, as a child, when she no longer showered with Errol and was banned from her parents' bed, it was the end of any touch contact with her parents except when they were angry with her.

Perhaps one of the reasons she clashed so much with her mother was that she was the one most like her. As a child many people commented on Joy's likeness to Mary's family; so much so that she went through a phase of thinking that as she bore no resemblance to her father she must be the product of an affair her mother might have had while her father was interstate or overseas with the Air Force. That would have given another reason for her to have not been wanted.

Many years later Joy learned that Mary's grand-father had been a convict sent from Ireland to Tasmania. Unlike many convicts, he had not become a model citizen on his release. He was a common criminal and not a political prisoner and he continued in and out of prison for a number of years in Australia for petty crime.

When a book was published with this information in recent years, Mary had commented, "You can't always trust all that is printed in these types of books." Joy knew this but was willing to trust a fair bit of what had been written this time. Her cousin who had researched the material was a stickler for accuracy. She had been a Director of Nursing in charge of an intensive care unit in the main city hospital and one of her hobbies was historical research. Joy had more confidence in her cousin's version of the truth than of her mother's.

Mary had told her daughters little of her father's history except that he was the first child to the second wife of her grandfather who had been in his sixties when her father was born in 1870. Had the shame of his past been a secret her mother had tried to keep? Was this why she had been so tough on Joy, punishing her so harshly, because she feared that she might end up in prison if she didn't? Had her mother thought she was so bad that this might be her fate? She had once stolen a small brooch from a shop when Mary refused to buy a present for her to take to the party. Perhaps this was an indication of how close to criminal she had come.

"I am hopeless. I should end my life. They would be better off without me," are thoughts that regularly surfaced for Joy. Many times she has contemplated killing herself but she couldn't bring herself to do it. Paul was a better person than she was, certainly a better parent. He had once told her jokingly, that he had his eye on a single woman who lived on a nearby farm and stood to get a good inheritance. "If anything happens to you," he said, "There's always Helen." it didn't feel like a joke to her. The irony of it was that if it had been her that died, he would easily have found someone else, where she never has.

Her children would have been better off without her shouting and hitting out at them. But she couldn't bring herself to end her life, such was her cowardice. When Paul died, Joy envied him and these feelings were fed as people told her how dreadful it was that such a good man should die so young and implied that if she had fed and cared for him better he might still be alive. On a logical level, she knew these thoughts were rubbish. The autopsy report began with the sentence, "This was a very healthy man," and also commented that cholesterol was not a problem. There seemed to be no indication of where the blood clot that caused his heart attack had come from.

Through the years that followed, she has continued from time to time to wish that she would die. She couldn't kill herself; that option had now been taken from her. It would be too cruel for her children to lose both parents, but if she could get cancer or some other socially acceptable way of dying then it would be okay, she thought. The children would cope. They had before. They would be better off financially and that would ease any pain for them.

It isn't easy being a single woman in a culture of couples. Sometimes you are sidelined and sometimes you are seen as a threat. Joy can't say how many people through the years have said to her, "So you've never remarried?" as if it were a choice. Some said it as if they suspected her of being gay because she had "chosen" to remain single.

When Paul died, she was working with four single women. One had been widowed in her early thirties, one had never married and two were divorced. Through the years she has worked with many other single women who would have married if they had had an opportunity. They sometimes said things to Joy, like, "If a man comes along, I get first choice because you have already been married."

Only five days after Paul's death, she thought that she could not live without a man in her life but she was soon to learn that in Australia, in the forty-to-sixty age group, there were eight times as many single women as there were single men. If a man became single in that time, he usually partnered again with a younger woman or went outside Australia to find a new wife. Because of the imbalance in numbers, the experience of an unattached man is very different from that of a woman as many women seek male companionship even if they don't want marriage.

Joy has swung between desperately wanting a partner, being glad that she doesn't have one and thinking that she mucked up her first marriage how could she ever cope with a second one. A cousin had a friend who lived three houses away. They did many things together but did not get in each other's way. This seemed an ideal arrangement to Joy.

Several women that she has met through the years who had re-married, told her that if the possibility ever arose, to consider it very carefully, especially if there were children on both sides as jealousies and conflict between the families seemed almost inevitable.

SEEING GOOD

"The easiest and noblest way is not to be crushing of others, but to be improving of yourself." Socrates.

Probably from the beginning of humanity, and certainly for several thousands of years, people have tried to explain why things happen from earthquakes and diseases to good crops and a plentiful supply of food. If the event was benevolent, they attributed it to the gods being happy. If what happened was malevolent then the gods must be angry. And if the gods are angry, who made them that way? Who is to blame for this disaster, large or small?

The answer generally was, and still is for many, that it was people or a person who is to blame. It's someone's fault. This is the way most of the world religions see things. Joy can remember people saying after Cyclone Tracey had hit Darwin that it was God's punishment for the heavy drinking of alcohol that went on in the city. It seemed a silly idea to Joy. She had struggled to see what was just in punishing all the children and those who did not live wild lives just because some did behave that way.

Joy has learnt that little is gained from trying to place blame. Once, to her shame, Joy had stood in her kitchen with tears streaming silently down her cheeks. She had been complaining yet again about something ten-year old Andrew had done. In response her neighbour had said gently, "Why don't you try to say something nice about him? He really is a good boy" Startled by these words she had replied, "I can't think of anything except what he does wrong."

Hearing these words out loud had hit her hard. It was only a few weeks since Paul had said, "Why, when there's fighting among the kids at football, do you always assume that ours are to blame?"

"Because they probably are," Joy had said. Could there be any doubt? She was always to blame for trouble among her siblings, or at least that was the impression she got from her parents. Try as she might, she never seemed to be able to do the right thing or be how they wanted her to be. She had always been in trouble. She had been told often enough that she was the bane of her parents' lives. She was to blame for the trouble. How could her children be any different?

She had been unaware of her habit of blaming her children but she did know that she alternately blamed herself for everything and blamed others entirely. Hadn't Annie recently said sarcastically, after she had been defending herself with excuses for yet another social faux pas, "You're never to blame, are you?"

Joy thought back to her childhood. Theirs was not a family given to praise for things done well. Try as she might to do the right thing, she never got it right. Once she had cut the lawn without having to be asked as a surprise for her father. When she proudly showed him, all he had said was, "Why didn't you pull out those weeds as well?" indicating an overgrown patch next to the lawn. So the next week she did pull out the weeds. One that she thought was a marshmellow proved particularly difficult to remove and she learned later that it was a prize hollyhock! If she hadn't known before, she knew then that she was a failure and that she would never get anything right. She had been shamed and she was ashamed.

In more recent years Joy has heard things like, "It takes twenty lots of praise and reassurance to overcome one criticism or put-down." Dr Phil on TV says that it takes two hundred times of saying, "You're okay" to counter one derogatory remark. As an adult, most of the 'put downs' she had heard came from herself. No one else needed to do it. She regularly told herself how hopeless she was.

When she was trying to find out about love, Joy learned that all children need to experience love, to have people who believe in them, to be able to behave in loving ways themselves. Joy realised that she had been loved by Mary's mother and Auntie Edna. They both helped her to feel special to them. Grandma belonged to a travel club that organised bus trips for one Sunday a month and she took Joy with her about twice a year, something none of the others got to do. Auntie Edna had Joy to stay sometimes in the school holidays.

Later, when Joy was studying interstate, her Grandma regularly sent her several dozen small cakes. There was excitement at the hostel when they arrived as they were shared around. One of the other girl's mothers sent her egg and bacon pies that were also shared. Auntie Edna wrote regularly and always included some very welcome money with the letter. When she came to stay briefly, she took Joy on a scenic helicopter ride and, when a few months later, her husband was in town, he took Joy to the Follies at the Tivoli, both experiences that she thoroughly enjoyed.

Joy began to think that if her parents were limited in their ability to love, it may well have been because they had only received limited love. It was likely that they too, hadn't known what it was to be unconditionally loved. Errol's parents were older when he was born. He had a nephew in the same squadron as he was during the War. He had once said that he had been brought up by the chamber-maid of their country hotel. Mary's father was mostly absent, leaving her mother with all the work and responsibility for the children. If she went back another generation perhaps she would find more explanations.

Taken to its ultimate conclusion, one could trace this right back to Adam and Eve, the primal parents. Did the buck stop there? Well, Joy didn't think so. If one went with the idea that allowed for them to get things wrong just as much as getting them right. She had thought about this before and realised that if people couldn't make decisions and therefore didn't had the ability to get things wrong, they would have to be robots and there wasn't much point to that!

Joy realised that our usual reactions to blame are to become defensive and to deny involvement or to become paralysed with guilt and shame. She saw that blaming focuses on the problem rather than on the solution, that when we are blaming others, we are avoiding taking responsibility for any part we might have had. We may also 'scapegoat' others by blaming them when they are innocent because we don't like them.

Many times we hear people say things like, "They had a choice so they only have themselves to blame. But although there may not be many situations in which people have no choice, there are a number of things that influence people's ability to make good choices such as the power of others involved and whether you have learned what is right or wrong for some behaviours. Joy didn't know she had a choice in some situations in her childhood. She had been beaten so often for involuntarily not complying with her parents' wishes that it is unlikely that she would choose to go against what they said.

Joy knows that it could be argued forever whether it is genetics or the environment that influences our decisions and how much of each it is. When she thought about her four grandparents and realised that she had eight great-grandparents and sixteen great-great grandparents she began to think that we are truly all mixed up and it's a wonder we aren't more of a mess. Discovering this has helped her become more compassionate. When Joy worked in the Young Offenders unit with three hundred and fifty young men, she would look across the yards and think, "What are your stories and histories? Didn't anyone ever love you? Were you all unwanted, uncared for?"

When a fifteen year old was charged with raping a woman in her eighties, people were saying that he was evil, that he deserved flogging or hanging. Joy wondered what it had been in his past that had led to this boy behaving in this way when every other fifteen year old would find the idea of behaving in this way abhorrent. If life hadn't been difficult for them before, it certainly was once they had a criminal record.

While Joy was still working with Community Health, she noticed that some old men had become obsessed by the War and all they wanted to talk about was their stories of the war. They seemed to have developed a need to tell others about it. They loved singing to songs that were popular around the time of the war and to look at photos and reminisce.

Then Errol started. Every time Joy visited, he would go on about the War; the times in the bombings of Darwin, in the jungles of Borneo and in Japan after the dropping of the bombs. He had been in Hiroshima. Mary was not patient with him and refused to listen so Joy made a point of letting him talk about it while she was there, hoping that he would spare Mary some of the details so she was less stressed. Eventually Joy learned that from the time he had come home after the War, every time there was thunder in the night, Errol would dive under the bed thinking they were being shelled. Mary, rather than sympathising with him, would be cross that he had disturbed her sleep and was behaving in an unmanly way. Errol was diagnosed as Post Traumatic Stress Disorder when he was being assessed for an Aged Care Facility nearly sixty years after the events that caused the condition.

It seemed to Joy that as the men became frailer physically they no longer had the strength to suppress the memories that they had kept hidden for so long. At the end of the war, they had been told to go home, forget what they had been through and get on with life. Much they were forbidden to talk about because of the Official Secrets Act. For the most part, they had managed to do this for forty or fifty years. Then these unwelcome thoughts came flooding back.

When Joy was reading a book on Holocaust Survivors it told of a psychiatrist who had noticed that he was seeing many Holocaust victims who began to have memories of horrific events emerging about forty years after the war. The Psychiatrist called this re-emergence of memories "The Holocaust Syndrome."

For Joy, this was good news. It seemed a likely explanation what she had noticed with the ex-servicemen and Lyn's returning memory. She has always been bothered by accusations of "False Memory". In recent times it has been a popular response to people reporting abuse many years later. It was a particularly popular theme in crime films and television shows for several years. The reaction by some to the disclosure when victims had finally plucked up courage to tell someone was that they had made it up. It had worried Joy until she had her memories legitimised in the conversation with Annie. It can be very painful to be doubted in this way and it was a relief to see the work of this psychiatrist who said that their memories were almost certainly legitimate.

Joy knows several people suffering from Post- Polio Syndrome. It was explained to her like this. These people had polio during the epidemic in the fifties. They recovered reasonably well and while some continued to have weakness in some muscles, others were able to get on with their lives appearing to be better, when, in fact, the damage was in part, still there.

They were able to live 'normal' lives but it took most of them more effort to do so and then, after many years and because of this extra stress, their bodies began to fail. They could no longer rely on these weary bodies to carry them and be for them what they had been. It has been said that they were just not as strong and resilient as those who had not suffered this disease but Joy likes to think that the fact that they did so well for so long shows that they may indeed be stronger and more resilient than most of us.

We accept this condition and are compassionate towards those whose lives are restricted as a result of this disease. Abuse has a similar impact on the minds and souls of those who have suffered from it. Most survivors of abuses manage to live productive lives but are experiencing more pain as they age and remember. This is especially so since sexual abuse has been so prominent in the media for several years now. Joy knows that there is less compassion for those who were victims of abuse or those who came from violent homes, who may be suffering again as they age; those whose lives have been violated by violence rather than viruses. She wonders if this could be because we somehow blame these people in ways that we would never blame the survivors of diseases like polio.

Joy began asking people her age, friends, acquaintances and some whom she met at breakfasts following Anzac Day Dawn Services, whether they saw that their father's War Service had affected their childhood. Many described how they lived with the anxiety of not knowing when their fathers would 'fly off the handle', of them drinking too much and of abuse of their mothers. They talked about being confused by their father's unpredictable behaviour and often thought that it was their fault. They tried to figure out what behaviours of theirs might trigger explosions from him so as to be able to prevent them happening. They also spoke of trying to avoid their fathers and to keep out of their way.

Some mothers were protective of their children in these situations but others seemed to struggle to keep their own heads above water themselves.

Recently Joy heard of research on mice which has suggested that second third and fourth generations of traumatised mice show heightened anxiety. The researcher suggested that it might be an advantage to explore this hypothesis in humans especially ones from abusive homes. Joy's response to hearing this was a resounding, "Yes, yes!" Since she began speaking to the children of returned servicemen she has felt anxious every time she hears that the government has sent troops overseas. "There go another X number of families whose lives will be changed forever by their parents' experiences."

BEING HERSELF

"Be as you wish to seem." Socrates

Probably ever since Joy subconsciously realised that she had not been wanted by her mother, she had been trying to become someone her parents would want. She didn't ask to be loved. That would have been too much to expect. Joy just wanted to be acceptable to her mother. It was the same with her father, especially after he stopped sexually abusing her. She did try very hard to be what she thought that they wanted but her efforts were in vain. It was confusing for her to hear people say that she should have been a boy or that she was a tomboy. Inside she would scream, "I am a girl; can't you see it?" Just because I'm not like the others doesn't make me not a girl!"

Joy tried to be what she thought her teachers wanted her to be but that wasn't a lot more successful. After she married she tried to be who she thought Paul wanted her to be, but this was another disaster. He wanted a traditional wife, organised, tidy, a good mother, and most of all, slim. Joy was never slim and Paul was disgusted when she put on weight with her first pregnancy. "No more children until you are back at the weight you were when we married." He said. Slowly she lost some weight. Luckily he left the birth control up to her and so before the target was reached, she was pregnant again.

In her mid-fifties, Joy realised that she had spent her entire life trying to be who she thought others wanted her to be and it had only ever partially worked! She set out to find out who she really was so that she could be acceptable to herself and that became quite a journey.

Joy realised that she has several pet hates among clichéd responses and reactions and in reflecting on small things like this she began to learn more about herself. Slowly she has come to accept herself and even like who she is. After Paul's death she got thoroughly fed up with people asking her how she was coping. "They don't actually want to hear if you are not coping. They want you to say that things are going okay and if you don't most quickly change the subject."

Her second pet hate is the use of the term "Closure." Joy is sure this word must have been dreamed up by someone who wasn't grieving or suffering in any way, to make him or herself feel better. Others want you to "get over it" because they feel uncomfortable with your suffering. Joy is convinced that everything that happens in our lives shapes us in some way, for better or worse or even both. Because of this, nothing can ever be completely signed off, because to do so would be to deny part of who you are. Complete closure cannot come until an individual ceases to be, as in death.

Joy also hates the question, "Are you a glass-half-full or a glass-half-empty person?" Her reply is that she is both and neither. She is neither an optimist nor a pessimist. She likes to think of herself as a realist who can be both optimistic and pessimistic at different times. Sometimes her glass in full to overflowing and sometimes it is almost empty. She states, "When we are all optimists, we tend to minimise harder issues and the suffering of ourselves and others. When we are pessimists, we see problems magnified and lose hope. Nobody can live without hope. The reality is that sometimes things do seem hopeless, too big for us to overcome. Then we need support and encouragement from others not condemnation for not behaving as they want."

Joy was rarely optimistic in the first half of her life and that reflects the reality of it. Her moods tend to swing rapidly up and down. For years when thinking about this, she has wondered if she suffered from Bipolar Disorder except that the experts say that in people with the disorder it takes months to transition from high to low and back again. Joy can do it in hours or even in minutes in some situations. She rarely tried to talk with a doctor about her depression even when it when on for months because there could be days when she was quite "high".

For her own understanding, Joy began to call her behaviour Rapid Cycling Bipolar Disorder and was surprised to find recently that there is such a condition. When she was in the library to look new books on abuse, she noticed a book on an end shelf. Called, "Scattered Minds", [Lenard Adler, G.P. Putman's sons, New York] it was written to offer "hope and help for Adults with Attention Deficit Hyperactivity Disorder." It says that most adults have lost the "Hyperactivity" component that is present in children displaying similar behaviour patterns and so fail to recognise the condition.

The first book that Joy read on this subject, having heard it reviewed on the radio about five years ago, was "Fast Minds" [Craig Surman, Tm Bilkey and Karen Weintraub, Berkley Books New York] and reading it was one of the most liberating things that has occurred in her life. It explained why she had so much trouble in conforming to expected behaviour. When Joy was young, Mary had taken her to a doctor because she couldn't cope with her; the doctor prescribed "Phenobarbitone" to calm her and Joy was kept on it for about eight years. It has recently been found to make hyperactive children even more active; paradoxical hyperactivity is how their behaviour is described.

Joy wondered why they had stopped giving it to her. Was it because it didn't seem to be working or because she had been beaten into an acceptable level of behaviour? She recently asked Mary about it but she could not remember. She recently turned a hundred and it is too late to bother her with questions. She was probably doing her best at parenting that she could do at the time.

What Joy learned from these books and many who know her well agree, that she conforms to the list of requirements to be classified as having Attention Deficit Hyperactive Disorder. As a child she was frequently in trouble for not sitting still and as an adult she has envied those who could do this. Once at a funeral she sat next to a woman whom she admired. The woman didn't move during the service. They were crammed into the church because there were many people present and Joy was conscious of wriggling and squirming the whole time.

Another thing was her inability to keep her mind on the subject in hand. Joy's head would be full of ideas and she would suddenly realise that her thoughts were miles from what was going on around her. This wasn't always such a handicap. When she was at University in her early fifties, she was petrified that this would lead her to saying something inappropriate in the tutorial groups. Once when she felt she had done something particularly bad, she plucked up courage to ask a lecturer she had come to trust. To her surprise he said, "It is really good when you have something to say or ask a question because while your comments and questions are always relevant to the subject, they are also always things the others have never thought about." This was encouraging but it also confirmed in Joy's mind that she was different from others and she didn't like to be different.

A third thing was that she had always felt socially clumsy. She would speak out of turn, say inappropriate things and interrupt. Oh how she interrupted! Joy knew it was wrong and rude but just couldn't seem to stop it especially when she was on a 'high'. All her New Year's Resolutions and prayers did no good. She would leave home for an outing promising, "Today I will listen and let the other person finish what they have to say," and all would go well for a few sentences and then with great shame, she would realise that she had done it again. She had cut the other person off in her enthusiasm to say something. Along with this is a tendency for her speech to get louder as she gets more enthusiastic or passionate about things.

Joy rarely drinks alcohol for fear of losing even more control and because her grandfather had been called alcoholic and she feared she might have an addictive personality.

All these things were part of the disorder. It was a relief to think that it was part of who she was and not because she had been deliberately naughty.

The book, "Fast Minds", had some good points to say about being this way. "These people," it said, "think outside the box and the community needs people with the ability to think outside the box." Wow! Only a few weeks earlier a long-time friend had said to Joy, "What I have always admired about you is your ability to think outside the box." That had been a special moment.

Back when she first heard about Edward de Bono and thinking outside the square she had thought that she would like to be able to do it and now, here was someone saying that she had always had that ability. She had indeed spent most of her life trying to comply with community expectations and stay within the box when it was a blessing to be outside.

This is not what the writer of "Scattered Minds" the other book on ADHD, is saying. His premise is that this condition is a disability that, fortunately, in his mind, can be alleviated by drugs. It can be treated with medication so we don't have to put up with people who interrupt us and fail to fit into the boxes we would like to put them in.

Attention Deficit Hyperactive Disorder now has DSM-IV recognition meaning that it has been classified as a psychiatric condition with recognisable criteria for diagnosis. Under these criteria there is no doubt that people who tick the right boxes on the check list are seen as "abnormal". Adler talks about the economic cost to the nation of the disorder. Perhaps "disorder" is correct in this case as these people find it very difficult to be orderly and organised. Joy wonders though, if our culture, communities and education systems could learn to nurture the strengths of people born this way [it is believed to be genetic] to benefit all people.

What of the benefits that de Bono proposed of being able to think outside of the square? Have they all been lost in the intervening decades?

The more Joy has thought about this aspect of who she is, the more she thinks that if a label is needed then a better one would be "Differently Able". She can understand that her behaviour has been frustrating to her parents and to teachers but in spite of all this, she has achieved huge amounts. She was not unintelligent just because she didn't learn as others do.

Joy has always had an insatiable desire to ask questions. This is what got her in to trouble so often as a child where unquestioning obedience was demanded. It translates into an appetite for new scientific knowledge. For her it is awesome and exciting. She knows that she can be a bore about it. She doesn't intend to convey that she knows more than others. She simply wants others to have the opportunity to marvel at new understandings and to ponder paradoxes and puzzles. Some might say a little knowledge is a dangerous thing but for Joy a little knowledge is often liberating from her former ignorance. She continues to delight in discussions and science shows.

The more Joy hears about things from matter billions of light years away to nano-technology the more amazing she understands that God must be. Her interest and excitement extends into areas of liberation and progressive theology and her learning is ongoing.

FINDING JOY AT LAST!

"I know that I am intelligent because I know that I know nothing."
Socrates

When Paul died, Joy felt all-consumed by the tragedy and wanted to tell everybody she met about it. It seemed in some way that she needed to verbalise what had happened to make sense of it. Her brain seemed incapable of processing the evidence she had. On one level, she knew only too well that this thing had happened. How could she *not* know with all the differences now in her life? But on the other hand part of her just couldn't comprehend how someone so healthy could be so alive one moment and dead the next. It helped to have others confirm that it wasn't just a nightmare; that it really had happened.

Joy considered the ways cultures had dealt with such grief in the past and thought that most of them would not be helpful for her. She certainly hadn't wanted to be burnt on a funeral pyre next to him! But she was now different in yet another way from most of her peers. Widows are supposed to be elderly. She found herself at some social functions, being seated with others more than twice her age. In some countries people in mourning wore black but she didn't look good in black and besides this, black had become the fashion colour so that most young people wear it which defeats the purpose of its being a sign of mourning. She heard of a country where widows wore their wedding rings on their other hand. She liked that idea. Then she wouldn't have to explain when people asked her about Paul but as it wasn't the custom here she would still have some explaining to do.

Perhaps it is a blessing that there are no outward signs to show that you are widowed. Some would say that it is good as the signs might lead to more discrimination. Perhaps, also, it is good that a person has come from an abusive home because if there was, they might be further abused by being blamed for what happened to them.

A colleague once asked to talk with her. The brother of a friend of his had been killed in an accident.

"He doesn't seem to be able to stop talking about it. It is very wearying. Is there anything you know of that we can do to help him?"

"My suggestion," Joy answered, "would be to intentionally listen to him and what he is saying. You may like to try saying something like, 'This whole incident must be very hard for you to get your head around,' or 'I have no idea how I would cope in this situation'." Often once a person realises they have been heard, they can stop verbalising it so much. Sometimes when people have told a painful tale, they will suddenly stop, feeling guilty for having imposed on the listener. Then say something like, "Well, I know that there are always others worse off."

Joy has a story she tells when people thought that they had complained too much about their pain. "Two people go to the Emergency Department of a hospital. One is having a heart attack and the other has a dislocated elbow. Obviously the person with the heart attack is worse off but the staff would not dream of saying to the one with the dislocated elbow, "Quit whinging! We are not going to help you because you aren't as bad." Her treatment might not be quite as urgent, but the medical staff know that if they were to send her away unhelped, she would be in pain and unable to live well for the rest of her life."

Joy had been told early when studying Occupational Therapy that everybody's pain should be treated with respect, whatever was causing it; she has tried to honour this even when she thought the other's pain was trivial. She knows how important it is to listen and be listened to. Once when Joy's younger son was fifteen, he was having a bit of trouble at school. She told a friend about this and her friend launched into detailed solutions for the problems. Joy had felt disempowered by the reply. She knew what to do about the problem. All she wanted was for her friend to say, "It must be difficult being a single parent to a teenage boy."

Joy had also learnt when she worked in Community Health to ask herself, "What might be behind what I am hearing? What is the hidden message this person is giving?" Over and over, elderly people would say things like, "My daughter never comes to see me." When Joy learned to ask, "When was she last here?" she found that she might be told, "Well, she was here yesterday." In this case the person was likely to be thinking, "She is not here as often as I would like her to be."

Joy comments that it has been important for her to learn to hear what is not said as a vital requirement for helping victims of abuse and family violence. For reasons of fear or shame, many find it difficult to admit, even to themselves, how bad things were or are. There is often no direct evidence of historic abuse.

When she was studying theology Joy was told that the absence of evidence is not evidence of absence. At that time they were talking about the absence of historical evidence for Biblical stories but it applies as much to accusations of abuse. The law requires evidence to prosecute in a criminal case and circumstantial evidence isn't generally good enough. "It would be his word against mine," is a reason many people give for not reporting the abuse the police. Victims of domestic violence and work-place bullying are now encouraged to keep a diary when possible, to verify their claims. Another reason is that people need to be strong enough to go through the court system. Although things have improved in these areas there is still a way to go.

Joy had several times seen on TV how people treated the accused. Police officers were going into a home to arrest a man. Outside his home were crowds of angry, self-righteous people were shouting, "Paedophile!" and hurling abusive words and anything else they could get their hands on. She wondered if her father would have been called a paedophile. If people had known, would they have behaved like this towards him? It took Joy many years to realise that if someone had gone to the police, this label may have publicly been put on her dad. Joy would not have wanted that.

Joy has only ever met one person whose father was imprisoned for sexual abuse and it had been that woman's mother who had been brave enough to go to the authorities. The daughter, now with children of her own, had long since lost contact with her father but she was a much more confident person than many of the other victims Joy has met.

"It was good to know that Mum risked so much for us. She lost her husband and his income and her status in society. She lost many friends who saw her as disloyal or as probably part of the problem. But we became a closer family and stronger in spite of the teasing at school when my father was imprisoned," she said.

It is often surprising to hear women say that they still love the person in spite of the treatment they have received from them.

When Joy worked in Occupational Therapy, she once had a client, a seven- year-old child who was classified as having multiple minimal disabilities. With a change of Government and financial cutbacks, funding had been withdrawn for help for the child with her schooling. The team of professionals looking after her was rightly upset. They were told that if she had one major disability, funding would have been retained.

The child's several minimal disabilities were arguably more of a handicap than a single major one would have been. What was more distressing was that most, if not all, of her disabilities could have been resolved with appropriate intervention at this age so that by adolescence she could have been functioning as well as any of her peers. Instead with the withdrawal of funding, she would almost certainly need assistance for the rest of her life.

It seemed to Joy that although this girl's disabilities were physical and intellectual, her story was a reasonable metaphor for many children from dysfunctional homes, who slipped under the radar and continued through life with multiple minimal handicaps from their experiences. They had multiple examples of "minimal damage" from their environment but those in authority failed to see the cumulative effect of this, instead concentrating on those with major problems. As a result, future generations were condemned to continue living and functioning at less than optimal levels at a continuing cost to the community.

Joy saw *Australian Story* on ABC TV, where a young cancer survivor had organised a photographic display of the scars that she and other young cancer sufferers bore on their bodies from where the tumours had been removed and from the effects of radio-therapy. They had decided to be proud of their scars and rather than trying to keep them hidden as seemed to be the instinctive thing to do. They had photographed them and had a display. They were proud that they had survived. They were saying to all who cared to come to the gallery, "These marks show what we have been through and survived. On one hand Joy felt that it was very brave of them to do this and on the other she envied them that they had such obvious scars to show for their struggle.

The week after this there was a programme about preventing Domestic Violence. A psychologist talked about the effects on the brain of a growing child of living in an abusive home; how it manifests in behaviour problems. Joy had just read that with new scanning technologies it is possible to get images of how people with Attention Deficit Hyperactivity Disorder brains work differently from ordinary brains.

She wondered if one day someone might scan the brains, hearts, spirits and souls of people damaged like her and put the result on display. She doubts that it will create much interest except among others with similar scars. Perhaps one day there will be such an exhibition to help people understand that injury does occur from abusive behaviour.

Abuse survivors' scars are not always obvious and generally they are not proud of them. If they are aware of them, they have tried to keep them hidden. But the scarring can cause problems, short circuiting the wiring of relationships. Joy thinks that it will be a long time before most of the survivors of abuse she knows would want to hold a public display of their wounds. Of course, if it would help prevent others from being damaged, they would probably reconsider.

Although Joy is generally seen as a friendly person, she has few close friends. She just hasn't been able to risk letting people getting close. They might find out how bad she is. She has seen herself as a fraud. She is better now but still gets anxious in social settings.

When Joy had been ordained eighteen years she had a conversation with someone who had been ordained for nearly thirty years and had recently had her fourth move to a new placement. Joy worked out that she had had three placements for a total of ten years and had done eighteen lots of supply. This is a highly unconventional path through ministry. She wondered if she had not gone to England for her first placement whether she would have had a more usual path. All the same, Joy is unsure that if she were given the chance to replay this part of her life, she would do it any differently.

"There are days when I simply cannot believe how my life has turned out," Joy says. "It is so different from what I expected when I was a farmer's wife living in the scrub. I still sometimes miss the smell of the sheep and the peace of the bush and the dream of my grandchildren on the farm."

Joy was told once of some researchers who were questioning people who had through significant bereavements. They all thought that they had grown and learnt from the grief experience and thought that they were better people now because of what they had suffered. Then they were asked if they would choose to go through such pain to become better people and they all said, 'No'. Joy could understand that. She would never have signed up to such a life but having now lived most of it, she is pleased with what she has learnt and how she has changed along the way.

Mary is still living independently. Joy grapples with whether she should say something to her about her childhood. Might there be something Mary would like to say if she gave her the opportunity or are Joy's thoughts of speaking to her, at her age, akin to revenge? This is a dilemma still to be resolved.

Somewhere along the line, Joy decided that the term 'survivor' no longer described how she saw herself. She was now a 'thriver'. She had achieved far above what she had ever dreamt that she might be able to and done all sorts of things that she had never imagined she could. Her relationship with her children has much improved and she was proud of how they are doing now as adults. Two are themselves parents much better parents than she had been. Paul had been a good father to them, never hitting or shouting at them as she had done and now his influence has paid off.

Lyn, Joy's youngest sister, has been a huge support and encourager of Joy for many years, especially since the death of Paul. A couple of years ago, when they were talking about the effects of grief, Lyn said to her, "You should write a book on loss. You have gathered thousands of stories of loss from your own experiences and through listening to others."

When she thought about it, Joy realised that her biggest sense of loss was about her own identity. Who was she, this strange person who although called "Joy" had little joy in her life until recent years? She saw, with a wry smile, that she hadn't liked herself much and that probably the person it was most important to get to know in an attempt to like more, was herself.

Recently memories were again stirred for Joy when she was involved in telling a group of people that a man who had been close to them for many years could no longer work with them as he was unable to comply with the conditions for getting a "Working with Children Certificate" because of his police record. The authorities seemed only concerned with the legal aspects of the situation and who might be sued if "anything happened". But Joy was more concerned about other possible victims. They had discovered that the man had two convictions a number of years apart.

The people were protesting so loudly about the action of the authorities that she feared for the health of any victim who may have been among them. She is sure that it is every bit as hard for a young person to disclose to an adult that they have been abused as it has been to disclose that they are gay. The people at the meeting were so strongly protesting on the man's behalf that Joy thought at one stage that they may have attacked her.

"They can't bring themselves to believe it is possible that their children may well have been a victim of this man," She thought. "I hope that none of them have been because it would be very hard for them."

Joy hopes that those who still hold the secrets of their abuse, and would like to speak with someone, can take courage from her to find a professional or self-help group to get started on the healing journey.

Many losses are unrecoverable, gone forever, but Joy, by encouragement, through risking, seeking and learning has found much of her true self and in doing so has become more loving and accepting and encouraging of others. It has been well worth the effort, pain and struggle of the journey.

Joy has lived in forty-eight different homes since Paul died. They shifted out of the farm-house into a smaller house when they put on an overseer who had eight children and some of the time when she was working for the Aged Care Assessment Team she lived in the town for several days each week to save on travelling as she had no one left to go home to.

Part of the time she was a student she did house sitting and then several times while she was doing supply that was extended, she was shifted to another house when the one she had first been given was needed. When she was in the ninth house she commented on that to Jess who said, "Mum, doesn't it say somewhere that if you give up your home you will receive one hundred more? I think that means you have ninety-one to go." [Mark 10:29].

There has been both joy and sadness for Joy in all the moves that she has had. Many times she has met people with whom she would like to be friends but after she has moved on, the energy required for settling in to a new place has meant that she has not been good at keeping up with those she has left behind. It is not always easy finding friends when you are new to the district. As one woman she approached put it, "I'm afraid I have all the friends I can cope with at present." It always seemed to prove just too difficult for her to settle into the new situation, keep up with her children and the rest of her family to work on continuing friendships. This is one of her biggest regrets.

What now of the lasting effects of having been sexually abused? Joy says, "I don't want to down-play it for other victims, but I am more sure than ever that it never occurs in isolation from other abuses and so to focus on one for healing and not acknowledge the others is to get only partial healing and restricted growth.

Both victims of abuse and abusers need help. It requires a huge effort on the part of society to change the culture that leads to all forms of abuse. I have seen over and over that when a person is encouraged, when their strengths are built upon, when they know that they are loved, they are far less likely to be abusive."

Joy recently commented, "I am grateful for most of my life experiences. Now that I am in my seventies, I can see that I have had full life; full of highs and lows, pain and joy, achievements and failures, excitement and boredom, some unique and some similar opportunities and experiences to hundreds of thousands of others. My life is now full of love. I can't believe how differently I see things from what I did forty years ago. Life is a real joy!"

Mary surrendered her driver's license when she was ninety-six. The girls had all been worried about whether she could see well enough to keep driving but no one was game to tell her to stop because they had seen what the loss of his license and independence had meant for Errol. Mary, though, quickly got the hang of using taxis, but with many of her friends now dead, she had fewer places to go. She now had nothing to do with her neighbours who were all less than half her age and so just before she turned ninety-nine she decided to move into a retirement village where she is doing well with plenty of people to talk with.

There is information on line about:

Where to go for help if you are a victim of domestic violence or abuse in any form.

Grooming and signs that a child might be being abused.

FORMS OF ABUSE

PHYSICAL: punching, hitting, beating, burning, choking, starving, neglect

PSYCHOLOGICAL: Manipulation, ignoring, jealousy

VERBAL : belittling, accusing, shouting

EMOTIONAL: teasing, ridiculing, love/hate

FINANCIAL: mean, over-control of spending, non-disclosure of spending

RELIGIOUS: ridicule, refusal to allow religious practice, over-control, compulsive observance.

SEXUAL: pressure to behave in any sexual way that you do not want. Being used as an object for another's sexual gratification in any way. Abstinence.

SOCIAL: isolation from friends, controlling of social life

REFLECTIONS ON EMOTIONS

Emotions, also spoken of as our feelings, are the reflex responses of the soul. They happen when certain buttons are pushed in our psyche. They spring out as expressions on our faces just like our lower legs swing out when a doctor strikes a certain spot with a little hammer. As a doctor can tell if the nerves in the leg are working properly by the response to the hit and then know how to proceed, so we rely in part on emotional responses to know how to proceed in relationships and social interactions.

In and of themselves, emotions are neither good nor bad. It depends on how we respond to them and use the energy released by them that matters. We cannot be fully-functioning humans without them and each one can be useful or harmful. For instance, shame keeps us behaving within boundaries that are acceptable for the smooth running of our communities but when taken to excess we see women who have been raped condemned to death because they are falsely blamed for having brought shame on their families.

Damage and diseases can mean that emotions shut down or become over-sensitive, either way making relationships more difficult.

Some theories say that there are really only two emotions, love and fear and that all others spring from one or other of these two. Emotions like anger and frustration, jealousy and envy come from fear and ones like joy and compassion come from love. We could not survive without fear. We need a healthy fear for self-preservation, so we don't put our fingers in electrical sockets or walk across busy roads or down dark alleyways at night alone. Nor can we survive without love. Babies totally deprived of love may develop personality disorders or refuse to eat to the point of starvation.

Emotions trigger the release of chemicals in our bodies that allow us to respond to the situation that has caused the emotion to arise. If it is fear, then adrenalin gives us the ability to fight or flee the situation. It is more likely, if anger accompanies the fear that you will choose to fight. You probably know all this, but one thing you may not realise is that fighting does not always have to be physical, fisticuffs type of stuff [or wars]. It can be channelled through non-violent protests and political action.

Emotions register as facial expressions in less than a second and it takes us more than that to control them and bring our faces back to bland if we want a classic poker-face. Most of us are able to pick up those split second changes and so know what others are feeling even if they try to deny it or when they may not have been aware of it themselves.

As with displaying and managing emotions, we can be poor, good or even hypersensitive in reading them on the faces of others. We may have been socialised against naming emotions such as anger so that it is difficult to admit to ourselves the strength of the emotion. Women may say we are cross or a bit upset rather admit to being furious.

Researches were surprised to find that we are born being able to feel shame. They are able to show that the muscles of babies only a few hours old withered when their mothers failed to smile at them and when strangers frowned at them. They lost eye contact and their heads drooped down and to the side as if to make themselves less visible, the classic shame response.

Many cultures maintain control in their societies by honour and shame systems. We may try to eliminate the discomfort of shame by shifting blame on to others. Taken to extreme it can result in the killing of others or of oneself. Self-loathing may not lead to a person physically killing themselves but rather it can cause us to behave in self- destructive ways such as under-eating, over-eating, taking unnecessary risks, withdrawing and refusing to take any of the risks that may lead to a fuller life.

"Unclean", "rotten to the core" and "from corrupted stock" were all expressions that Joy had heard used to describe people and she wondered if they referred to her, especially since at Sunday School they were told they were all wretched sinners. [This is now classed as abusive]

It is important for us to understand our emotions to know ourselves and to have good relationships with others. Many of us grew up in a time when it was considered weak or ill-mannered to display our emotions and so we were stunted in this aspect of who we are.

In recent times a number of good books have been written on emotional intelligence which help people understand their feelings better.

FIGHT, FLIGHT OR FACE AND FIX

Most people are familiar with the fight or flight concept where it is said that when we are faced with a threat, we either fight that which is threatening us or we flee from it. Our bodies produce adrenaline to give us the energy necessary for whichever of these two we choose. Sometimes when we are unable to physically flee, we do so mentally, by denying that the problem exists, by dissociating in our minds from what is happening [multiple personality syndrome]. This can be how children block out abuse.

However, sometimes these memories can come back. When they resurface or when we have becomes older or stronger, we can choose to deal differently with the abuse or with the memories of it.

Always remember that there are professionally trained people who can help you with this.

The first thing is to face the issue.

This may require admitting that what is or was happening is abuse and not just something a bit awkward, embarrassing or uncomfortable or something everybody endures. It is likely to be illegal, unethical and immoral. It is not wrong to have wanted it to stop and to want the perpetrator punished. It is a good thing if the action you take causes the person to reconsider their actions and to cease abusing. It may help to take the abuse more seriously if you ask yourself, "If I heard of this happening to someone I love, would I let it continue or go unreported?"

This is also about not taking the abusers word about who is or was responsible for the behaviour. Abusers often seek to put the blame on their victims, telling them such things as, "If you hadn't... I wouldn't have..." or "You were acting in such a way that I couldn't help myself." Children cannot be held responsible for the actions of an adult, nor a vulnerable woman for the actions of a more powerful man. In other words, however anyone is behaving, no one else has the right to ab-use her/him.

The second thing is to keep yourself or those involved safe from future abuse.

This means reporting abuse of children to the police.

Where you are the victim, it means looking after yourself which may be a new and difficult idea. It is not known whether some people become vulnerable because their self-preservation instincts are less sharp or their instincts are less sharp because they have been abused but it is important to learn to trust what your gut is telling you about someone and plan a way of protecting yourself if necessary. Ask, "What would it take me to get out of this situation?" "What would be the action on his part that I absolutely could no longer tolerate?" "When will I be ready to say, 'For the sake of everybody involved, I will not tolerate this any longer'?"

Authorities advise victims to disengage as early as possible. The first time you are abused is the time to address the issue. Many people don't act in the hope that things will improve but they rarely do in spite promises from the abuser that it will never happen again.

Professional help can be essential at this time. It may be necessary to plan to remove some of your possessions slowly from the home to safe keeping over several months in readiness to leaving.

Having a plan of action will be strengthening for you.

The third thing is to also plan growth/ healing for yourself. This includes, if possible, ensuring that others aren't being abused by this person. This can mean making a report to the police. It can take a lot of strength and resolve to do this but don't be put off by that. The police services are much more sensitive to such complaints than they used to be and more supportive of victims even when it just seems to be your word against his. It can be that someone else has complained about the same person and your report will help them build a case.

For some people, joining a group of survivors for short or long term can be helpful in getting your abuse into perspective. Knowing that there are others who understand through having experienced something similar themselves can be liberating.

On the other hand it is okay if you just want to forget about it and can't face hearing others talking about what happened to them. Do what is right for you! When you were being abused, you didn't have that freedom of choice. Now you do; look after yourself!

You may feel that what happened to you wasn't really significant, that there are others worse off than you, so it's not worth doing anything about your pain. Joy tells this story. "Two people went to an emergency room at the hospital. One had been in a major accident and had head injuries and broken bones. The other had a dislocated elbow. Obviously one was worse than the other but the ER room would never send the second one away without attending to her pain. If they did she would suffer for the rest of her life. Physical pain, whatever its cause, is taken seriously and we need to take emotional pain seriously as well and ask those best trained to assess it for us and help us with it rather than just putting up with it year after year.

Many people in our communities are in pain because of the wear and tear that has occurred on their joints. The reason why most of them seek joint replacement surgery is to alleviate the pain they are suffering and to become more mobile and independent again.

To reach the point of less pain or no pain requires going through pain, the pain of the surgery and rehabilitation, the frustration of maybe weeks of being dependent on others and unable to get to your usual social events. But it is almost always worth it in the end. Thousands of people go through this each year, especially as they get older. We are prepared to do this for our physical comfort, why not also for our psychological well-being?

QUESTIONS FOR SURVIVORS

Do I want to move on from where I am with this issue?

How have I coped with the memories I have of abuse?

What ways have been positive and what has been self-defeating?

Am I ready to speak with a professional person, counsellor, police?

If so do I have a friend/support person who I would like to go with me initially?

Can I name the feelings I have surrounding the abuse I suffered?

What is behind these feelings?

How do I usually deal with these feelings and what might be a better way of doing it?

Do I want to face these things now and if not when might I be ready?

If I am in an abusive relationship now, what would be the last straw that would trigger my exit?

What do I need to organise for this?

In what ways can I be kind to myself and improve the way I speak to me?

In what ways am I proud of myself and what I have achieved?

What are my worst fears in speaking about the abuse?

What would be a good outcome for me?

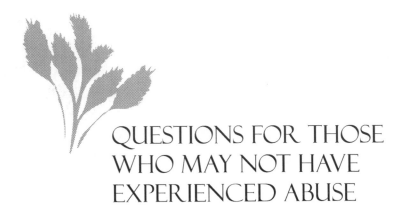

QUESTIONS FOR THOSE WHO MAY NOT HAVE EXPERIENCED ABUSE

What has surprised you in this story"

What issues has it raised that you have not thought of before"

How have you previously felt when you have heard the stories of victims?

Has this changed and why?

How do you think that you would respond if someone you had known and trusted all your life was accused of sexual abuse?

What are your thoughts on the idea that abuse is much broader than sexual abuse?

How could you support a victim or victims through recovery to become thriver?

How do you plan to learn more about these problems and the impact on our communities?

HELPFUL SUGGESTIONS TO MOVE TOWARDS HEALING FROM VIOLENCE, ABUSE AND LOSS

We accept that physical healing takes time and can be more painful before it gets better. Never-the-less, we choose to go through the immediate pain so things will be better in the future. So it may be for recovery from the trauma of abuse. It may not be easy to go through the counselling necessary but it will be worth it in the end for the freedom it brings.

Part of your recovery can be to organise a celebration, ceremony, or a rite that will have significance for you. You may like to do different things at different stages of your recovery and growth.

COMPOST AND POT PLANT

Write or otherwise depict the abuses you have suffered on paper.

Tear the paper into tiny scraps and add it to manure and plant matter, to make compost.

Place this in a pot and plant a perennial flower or shrub, to represent yourself, in the pot.

This symbolises that the abuses you experienced can be used to help you grow stronger. They will always be part of who you are but are now you are taking control of your pain and can use it for your benefit.

VERBALISING YOUR STORY

It may be easier for you to make sense of what has happened by talking about it to a professional person such as a doctor, psychologist, or counsellor working with centres for victims of abuse. As you hear your words the reality of your situation becomes clearer for decisions to be made.

Don't be discouraged and give up if the first person you try to talk with cannot hear what you are saying. Try someone else. Doctors can refer you to a psychologist covered by Medicare for several visits.

PEELING THE ONION or REVEALING
THE HEART OF THE ROSE.

These two images have a similar outcome. They are about gradually peeling away layers of life to reveal what is at the heart or core.

Florists sometimes take a barely opened bud and slowly and gently fold back the delicate petals so that the flower is more open.

It is not unusual for survivors of abuse to recognise that they over react to some present situations without knowing why this happens. Joy described such times for her. "Everything would be fine and then something would happen and I would immediately fly off the handle. It was like an anaphylactic reaction over which I had no control. When I began to ask, 'When have I felt like this before?' I was able to understand the strength of my reactions. It was often because I felt threatened in some way because of past experiences. When I accepted the reality of my reactions and the cause, things got better and in time my reactions lessened considerably."

We can do a similar thing using feelings to gently go back to what is at our core, step by step.

When you identify when you have felt this way and why you can then deal appropriately with what you have discovered by talking to a professional, a friend, journaling, or any other of the techniques suggested.

RITES AND SERVICES

Develop a ritual for private use, or for use with a group of friends, or for a religious service that will help you symbolically in some way.

The ritual may include expressions of:-

Lament: deep sorrow, despair.

Traditionally expressed with ashes, wailing, tearing of fabric and /or salt water representing tears.

Anger: may be expressed by pounding a drum or cushion, controlled burning of a significant or symbolic item, or screaming.

Shame: there is much wrong with me. I cannot be loved.

Write a letter to yourself to tell your inner being that you love and understand her/him and point out at least five of the best things about yourself. Give yourself permission to buy yourself some flowers or treat yourself in another way such as getting a cuddly toy to show you inner child she/he is loved and accepted as they are. Buy a special box in which you can keep cards, letters and tags from gifts of flower that indicate that you are loved. Go through these things when you are feeling unloved or alone.

Guilt: I have done something [or many things] wrong.

Write what you have done on paper to be burnt. Seek to admit the wrong-doing to the person violated and consider what can be done as restitution and do this if possible.

If you feel unclean from what has happened, the ritual could include water and symbolic washing using special aromas and being wrapped in beautiful soft towelling.

Indigenous people use smoke to cleanse and when I was a child the health authorities used fumigation to cleanse. You could borrow this idea adapting it for yourself using incense.

If the abuse took part in darkness your ritual could include candles to symbolise light and you could get yourself a new bedside light as a sign of a new start.

If helpful to you and possible you may like to have a private religious service, maybe in your home, at a retreat centre, in a national park or at a beach.

You may like to include an element of thanks to those who have helped you in your journey.

LIGHTENING THE BURDEN
OF UNHELPFUL COMMENTS.

When you disclose that you are a survivor of abuse, some people respond with hurtful or accusing comments like, "You must have known it was wrong. Why didn't you tell someone! Or Why didn't you just leave?"" These can cause you to feel angry, indignant, ashamed or a number of other ways. Here is a way of helping with those feelings.

Take a large sheet of brown paper about two metres by one point five metres. You can put it on the floor or on a table.

Take a thick red felt tipped pen, carpenter's pencil or something similar.

Write on the paper things that had been said to you that were NOT helpful.

Some of the unhelpful things are, "Children forget," "You should be over it by now," "You must forgive." "You'll get married again; there are plenty more fish in the sea," or "You can have another child."

These things are often said by well-meaning friends who had no idea how much their comments hurt.

Screw the paper into a tight ball and kick or throw it around. When you run out of energy, the ball can be consigned to a bin for recycling into cardboard or used to start a fire.

LIST OF LOSSES

Suffering abuse always robs the victim, taking from them such things as innocence, trust, security, virginity, control of their lives. It causes major and chronic loss.

Major losses are always complex, complicating the grief process. We need to be realistic about the magnitude of our losses and gentle with ourselves through the recovery time.

Write a list of everything that you have lost through the abuse.

You may like to do it pictorially by painting a picture of a pond where the water has been disturbed where a stone has landed.

Name your major loss at this centre point. Then on the ripples around, going out from the centre, write, draw or in some other way signify your other losses.

You may need a series of pools.

You may be able to think of a different way of expressing this.

If you are up to this stage, you may like to draw some flowers, trees, or animals around the pond and write the gains you have made on these signs of life.

MOSAICS

Many victims feel quite rightly, that their lives have been shattered by what happened.

Sometimes it is helpful to make something beautiful out of shattered pottery and tiles to represent how lives do not need to remain in pieces but can be put back together to become attractive and useful.

The mosaic shows that that which was shattered will never be the same again; that that which has happened has altered you. The aim is not to put the object back in its original state like Humpty Dumpty. It is not trying to pretend that this thing never happened but aiming to demonstrate that it need not be the end of a beautiful life.

Choose a design that has some significance to you, depicting healing and growth. You may like to make a wall plaque for the garden, a tabletop, or plate, or even the surrounds for a fountain.

BROKEN GLASS can represent SHATTERED LIVES

This is similar to the previous suggestion.

When Joy was living in England there were many small pieces of broken glass in several colours, on the beach near which she lived. These pieces had been tumbled in the surf and against the rocks until all the rough edges have been made smooth. She collected some and other similar pieces of glass from Australian beaches since her return and now has them in a clear glass jar on a display shelf. A number of people have commented on the collection which gives her an opportunity if she wishes to explain their significance to her.

The thought of the shattering of the bottles reminds her of the damage done in many people's lives but these pieces remind her that the rough and tumble of every-day life can over time, wears away the jagged parts of damage that could injure us further. Some of the pieces have already been turned into things of beauty at workshops Joy has run and can be used in a similar way to mosaic pieces.

It is fun collecting these pieces.

STAINED-GLASS

Some survivors feel that they have been left with a stain on their character following the events of their lives.

Stained-glass forms the basis of some of the most beautiful creations in the world and are precious to many people with their strong colours and vibrant stories. Stained is NOT the same as spoiled!

You might like to make your own stained glass window. Sometimes there are classes in the district.

It you don't have access to actual stained glass, you may like to make one with alternate materials.

You can start small by using simple shapes like a rectangle or a star. Plan it on paper with coloured pencils or felt tipped pens.

A similar effect can be made from cellophane and cardboard, coloured craft paper [if it doesn't need to be transparent] or felt or other fabric and made into a quilt or wall hanging.

There may be classes in stained glass work or you may be lucky enough to have a stained glass artist in your district who could help you to make one from actual stained glass or you could commission for your home to remind you of your inner beauty and strength.

MEDITATION

Many people find meditation helpful and there are a number of places that teach the techniques such as centres of Spirituality and Retreat Centres.

JOURNALLING

Keeping a journal is another way of coming to terms with your life's journey. As you reflect on your writings, perhaps weekly, it helps you see the reality of your life with all its highs and lows.

It is a helpful way of developing your spirituality.

Some people like drawing or painting in their journals, others add photos and other small mementoes such as dried flowers or small pieces of fabric.

If you are going to be realistic about your life, you will want to write about difficulties, problems and pain as well as good times and achievements. This is legitimate and being honest about where you are at.

Try to recognise and name five good things that have happened for you or five beautiful or fascinating things you have noticed each day to feed your soul. Don't be discouraged if you find this hard to begin with. It is likely to get easier as you go on.

POETRY

Writing poetry can be helpful either as part of journaling, or on its own, for private satisfaction or for sharing. It is up to you.

Find poems that you enjoy and that are empowering and add them to your journal.

You may like to write it as an autobiography as Joy has done.

Printed in the United States
By Bookmasters